INVOCATIONS and BENEDICTIONS for the Revised Common Lectionary

COMPILED AND EDITED BY

John M. Drescher

Abingdon Press
Nashville

Library of Congress Cataloging-in-Publication Data

Invocations and benedictions for the Revised common lectionary /
compiled and edited by John M. Drescher.
    p.   cm.
    Includes index.
    ISBN 0-687-04629-7 (pbk.: alk. paper)
    1. Prayers. 2. Invocation. 3. Benediction. 4. Common lectionary
(1992) I. Drescher, John M.
    BV245.I687   1998
    264'.13—dc21   97-42472
                                                          CIP

Contents

Introduction

....

Invoking or inviting God into the presence of God's people as they worship, as well as pronouncing a benediction or blessing upon these people as they leave the worship of the sanctuary, is a sacred honor and precious privilege.

The invocation and benediction should convey the glory, goodness, and richness of fellowship with God and God's people, the opening of all of life to Christ, who promises his presence wherever and whenever people meet in his name. These elements of worship should convey the privilege of going forth with renewed faith, to live by the guidance and power of the Holy Spirit.

The invocation can and should be one of the most significant elements in a service of worship. The very name of the prayer, *invocation*, portrays the nature of what is sought. It is a simple, humble, quiet, earnest invitation for God to be present with the assembly. The invocation should also lead each worshiper in voicing the heart's desire for God's presence and blessing.

The benediction has also been an important part of worship. It conveys the pronouncement of God's presence and blessing upon the worshipers as they leave the worship service. The benediction should have a commissioning quality—a sending of believers forth, strengthened by God, to face the world, in the week ahead, as witnesses to the living Lord and Savior.

To aid in all of this, these invocations and benedictions have been prepared. Each one can be used as written, or can be readily adapted by the worship leader to more closely fit the needs of individual congregations.

An effort was made, as much as possible, to tie the invocation and benediction to one of the scriptures of each Sunday's lectionary reading. Also, it seemed important to keep alive those great benedictions from the Scripture such as

Numbers 6:24-26; 1 Kings 8:57, 58; Romans 15:5, 6, 13, 33; 2 Corinthians 9:8; 13:14; 1 Thessalonians 5:23, 24; Hebrews 13:21, 22; Jude 2:24, 25; and Revelation 1:4-6. In addition, readers will note the inclusion of a separate section devoted to special days of the Christian year.

Year A

Advent Season

....

First Sunday of Advent

Lections: Isaiah 2:1-5; Psalm 122; Romans 13:11-14; Matthew 24:36-44

Invocation

Eternal and most holy God, we praise and honor you as we gather in the name of your dear Son, Jesus. During this Advent season we sense your nearness in the songs we sing and in the words we hear from holy Scripture.
May your light and peace radiate about us and within us as we worship you today. We praise and thank you for this house of worship and this body of your church. In expectation and joy, we worship you now and each day until Jesus returns to claim his own. In the name of Jesus, we pray. Amen.

Benediction

Go in anticipation of God's grace and mercy. Go in anticipation of Jesus' love and forgiveness. Go in anticipation of the Holy Spirit's presence in comfort and hope. Go in peace. Amen.

Second Sunday of Advent

Lections: Isaiah 11:1-10; Psalm 72:1-7, 18-19; Romans 15:4-13; Matthew 3:1-12

Invocation

O Lord, our God and Savior, come among us.
In this worship hour,
Open our minds to understand your purpose for each of us,

Open our hearts to make a ready response to your voice.
Give us understanding of your will, and the courage and commitment to follow Jesus, who said, "I am come to do your will, O God."
May we heed the message to repent and bring forth fruits that show true repentance.
Increase our love for you, O God, and for one another, we ask through Jesus Christ our Lord.

Benediction

"May the God of steadfastness and encouragement grant you to live in harmony with one another, in accordance with Christ Jesus, so that together you may with one voice glorify the God and Father of our Lord Jesus Christ" (Rom. 15:5-6).

Third Sunday of Advent

Lections: Isaiah 35:1-10; Psalm 146:5-10 or Luke 1:47-55; James 5:7-10; Matthew 11:2-11

Invocation

LEADER: Happy are those whose help and hope is in the Lord.

PEOPLE: **Our help rests in you, O God,**

LEADER: The one who made heaven and earth, the sea and all things in the sea,
The one who executes justice for the oppressed,
And gives food to the hungry.

PEOPLE: **Our hope rests in you, O God,**

LEADER: The one who sets the prisoners free,
And opens the eyes of the blind.
The one who lifts up those who are bowed down,
And watches over the strangers.

ALL: **We come hoping, O God. Help us. Amen.**

Benediction

Go and tell what you have seen and heard.
The blind receive their sight, the lame walk,
The lepers are cleansed, the dead are raised,
The deaf hear, and the poor receive good news.
Blessed are you who have eyes to see and ears to hear.

Fourth Sunday of Advent

Lections: Isaiah 7:10-16; Psalm 80:1-7, 17-19; Romans 1:1-7;
Matthew 1:18-25

Invocation

In this special season of Advent
We come to you, O God.
Give us a vision
Not just of a baby in Bethlehem's barn,
But of the Lord of Lords;
Not only of a lad in Nazareth,
But of the hope of the world;
Not only a rabbi teaching on a hillside and in a temple,
But the revealer of yourself;
Not only one who climbed a cross,
But one who was raised to life,
Who lives forevermore,
Our hope of life everlasting,
Jesus Christ our Lord and Savior.

Benediction

Go from this place
And may Christ,
Emmanuel, God with us,
Go with you this day, and always.

11

Christmas Season

First Sunday After Christmas Day

*Lections:*Isaiah 63:7-9; Psalm 148; Hebrews 2:10-18; Matthew 2:13-23

Invocation

Lord Jesus Christ, we are again in the throes of celebrating your birth and life among us.
Revive in us the wonderment of Mary and Joseph, living with the miracle and day-to-day practicality of life with you.
Renew in us the dedication of the Magi who sought long and hard to present you with your first birthday gifts.
Receive from us abundant honor and love, our Savior and our God. Amen.

Benediction

May the birth of Jesus reverberate anew throughout your world with joy.
May the Spirit of Jesus guide all of your words and thoughts with love.
May the life of Jesus inspire you to follow his ways of peace, until the whole world is, again, full of his glory.

Second Sunday After Christmas Day

Lections: Jeremiah 31:7-14 or Sirach 24:1-12; Psalm 147:12-20 or Wisdom of Solomon 10:15-21; Ephesians 1:3-14; John 1:(1-9), 10-18

Invocation

Today we rejoice, O God
That you revealed yourself in Christ,

Creator, Redeemer, Sustainer,
As your Word became flesh.
Reveal Christ to us today
As we gather—
Those who, by the power of the gospel,
Have become your children—
The children of light.

Benediction

Go forth as children of the light
Shine forth in the darkness.
Let the gospel become flesh in you.
And may the love, peace, and joy of Christ
Radiate from your life.

Season After the Epiphany

Baptism of the Lord
(First Sunday After the Epiphany)

Lections: Isaiah 42:1-9; Psalm 29; Acts 10:34-43; Matthew 3:13-17

Invocation

O God, as we join in worship,
Open our eyes to behold wondrous things out of your Word;
Open our ears to hear what the Spirit is saying to the church;
Open our hearts to believe unto salvation and righteousness;
Open our lips to witness to our living Lord, Jesus.
In whose name we pray. Amen.

Benediction

Go and speak as God has spoken to you.
Go and forgive as God has forgiven you.
Go and love as God has loved you.
Go and become as God has directed you.
Go and live as Christ has commanded you.
And go with God's blessing,
Live in God's will,
And God will be with you. Amen.

Second Sunday After the Epiphany

Lections: Isaiah 49:1-7; Psalm 40:1-11; 1 Corinthians 1:1-9; John 1:29-42

Invocation

Welcome, welcome to the Christ
  Chosen by God to reveal himself
  Who came as a servant
    To restore the tribes of Jacob;
    To bring salvation to the ends of the earth.
Welcome to the Holy One
  The one in whom we can put our trust
  Who hears our cry
  Who puts our feet on a firm place
  Who gives a new song in our hearts
  Whose righteousness we proclaim.
Welcome, welcome to those who come to worship him.

Benediction

Lord, we gathered to worship you,
  The one who gives a new song and plants our feet on a firm place.
  We put our trust in you.
  Continue to challenge us as we accept the revelation of yourself through Jesus. Empower us by the Holy Spirit to daily give witness of our relationship with you. Through Jesus Christ, our Lord.

Third Sunday After the Epiphany

Lections: Isaiah 9:1-4; Psalm 27:1, 4-9; 1 Corinthians 1:10-18; Matthew 4:12-23

Invocation

Lord, it is winter now. The days are short, the darkness of our despair encroaches soon. . . . Still, you call us out of this darkness into your great light.

The winds of our icy discontent swirl all about us, to freeze our faith and numb our courage . . . but you are our light and salvation, why should we be afraid?
God, enter with us into this place, your house. Here, may all that troubles us melt in the light and warmth of your care.

Benediction

Go now into this cold world, warmed by the very presence of God.
Go in safety, for there is no place that God has not already been.
Go in joy, for Jesus has already gone ahead of us, and we gladly follow.
Go in confidence, for we are kept in God's care.

Fourth Sunday After the Epiphany

Lections: Micah 6:1-8; Psalm 15; 1 Corinthians 1:18-31; Matthew 5:1-12

Invocation

O God, we come to this place of worship. We invoke your presence.
We come inquiring of you, our God, Where is the wisdom that comes from you? Where is true living? Where is your blessing to be found?
We come to you the author of wisdom, and the source of life. In our own way and in our own time, speak to our hardest questions and to our deepest needs.
As we quiet ourselves in your presence, and bow ourselves before you, we ask that you will look into our hearts, listen to our thoughts and intentions, review our daily actions, and speak to us of your wisdom, your justice, and your kindness. Speak to us of your righteousness and sanctification and redemption.
Show us the way to walk with you, our God.

16

Benediction

Blessed are we who have heard the Word of the Lord, and blessed are we who have seen both the wisdom of God and the foolishness of God. Blessed are we who have received life through the foolishness of God's extravagant love, which our God demonstrated by sending Jesus to be our Savior and Lord. Through the new life continually being created in us, let us go forth to do what is just among our neighbors; go forth and faithfully love the people we meet this coming week; go forth to live in humble fellowship with our God. Through Jesus Christ our Lord. Amen.

Fifth Sunday After the Epiphany

Lections: Isaiah 58:1-9*a*, (9*b*-12); Psalm 112:1-9 (10); 1 Corinthians 2:1-12, (13-16); Matthew 5:13-20

Invocation

O God, in this hour we pray.
We invite your presence.
What we know not, teach us,
What we see not, show us,
What we have not, give us,
What we are not, make us,
Through Jesus Christ, our Lord. Amen.

Benediction

Go from this place of united worship
Strengthened by the Spirit in your inner being,
So that you, at all times,
In all things,
Wherever you are
May be enabled to do God's work
In the power of the living Christ. Amen.

Sixth Sunday After the Epiphany

Lections: Deuteronomy 30:15-20 or Sirach 15:15-20; Psalm 119:1-8; 1 Corinthians 3:1-9; Matthew 5:21-37

Invocation

We invite your presence today, O God.
We come to you, our God, and Creator,
As children,
As those growing to maturity,
In whom you are at work,
Through your Word and Spirit,
To make us servants of Christ and vessels
for your service,
Created for your glory.

Benediction

Go as God's children,
Remember the words spoken here,
Review the hymns sung here,
Recall the prayers prayed here,
Rely on the fellowship known here,
Reverence the Savior worshiped here,
Recollect the blessings found here,
Respond to the Spirit met here
Until, by God's grace, we return here.
Through Jesus Christ, our Lord.

Seventh Sunday After the Epiphany

Lections: Leviticus 19:1-2, 9-18; Psalm 119:33-40;
1 Corinthians 3:10-11, 16-23; Matthew 5:38-48

Invocation

Come among us O God,
And manifest yourself to each person present.
Show us the Lord Jesus,
As the only foundation for our faith.
Make real to each of us
The truth that we are your temple,
Your dwelling place,
The home of your Holy Spirit.
We pray this in Jesus' name.

Benediction

Go forth from here today
Indwelt by the Holy Spirit,
Made holy and kept pure,
Strengthened and sustained,
Guided and filled,
By the very Spirit of Jesus Christ.

Eighth Sunday After the Epiphany

Lections: Isaiah 49:8-16*a*; Psalm 131; 1 Corinthians 4:1-5;
Matthew 6:24-34

Invocation

Our Lord and God. Yearning, broken, burdened with worry,
we come to be reverently still before you. In this place of
refuge there is calmness. In this place of healing there is
hope. In this place of worship there is joy.
Restore our souls as we kneel in spirit before you. Restore
our being as we take hope in your promises. Restore our
dignity as we rejoice in our salvation.

19

Benediction

Having been here we've met with the Lord. As we go from here may we go with the Lord. Take God's Spirit and Word to linger on in our hearts and to guide us in the coming days. We've been touched by restoration and refreshed through a renewed spirit: enlightened, encouraged, and strengthened for having worshiped together.
And now may the mercy, grace, and peace of our Lord Jesus be with us.

Ninth Sunday After the Epiphany

Lections: Deuteronomy 11:18-21, 26-28; Psalm 31:1-5, 19-24; Romans 1:16-17; 3:22b-28, (29-31); Matthew 7:21-29

Invocation

Come among us, O God.
Reveal your will.
Give to each of us
That inward grace, courage, and wisdom
To not only say, "Lord, Lord,"
But to do your will, O Christ.
Only then shall we withstand
The stress and floods of life,
And go from here
Better because we have been here.

Benediction

"The LORD our God be with us,
as [God] was with our ancestors;
may [God] not leave us or abandon us,
but incline our hearts to [God],
to walk in all [God's] ways, . . .
to keep [God's] commandments,

[God's] statutes, and [God's] ordinances,
which [God] commanded our ancestors." (1 Kings 8:57-58)

Last Sunday After the Epiphany
(Transfiguration Sunday)

Lections: Exodus 24:12-18; Psalm 2 or Psalm 99; 2 Peter 1:16-21; Matthew 17:1-9

Invocation

Lord God, we meet as your people,
Redeemed by Jesus Christ.
Make us eyewitnesses of your glory.
Give us ears to hear
Your voice from heaven.
May the Holy Spirit,
Who speaks of Christ,
Who shows us Christ,
Who magnifies Christ,
Give us a fresh vision of Christ,
Today.

Benediction

Go forth from here,
And, having seen the Lord of glory
On the mountain of worship and praise,
Go into the valley of life,
Knowing that the Lord of glory
Goes with you
In the presence and power of his Spirit
Who dwells within you.

Lenten Season

....

First Sunday in Lent

Lections: Genesis 2:15-17; 3:1-7; Psalm 32; Romans 5:12-19; Matthew 4:1-11

Invocation

Gracious God and Lord of all, we gather in your name, and invoke your presence. Surround us with your steadfast love in order that we may no longer hide in fear. We are all too aware of the death in our lives—of the sins that ensnare us while promising us life; of the tempter's traps that lead us away. Surely, Lord God, your grace is much more abundant than the evil that tempts us. Rain down on your children, with the mighty waters of your grace. May we be sheltered under your arm and preserved in your love. Our trust is in you, through your Son, Jesus Christ. Amen.

Benediction

Happy are those whose sins are covered,
Whose transgressions are forgiven.
For great is the free gift of grace
And great is the love that surrounds those who trust in the Lord.
Receive then this gift of grace and walk in the way of love.

Second Sunday in Lent

Lections: Genesis 12:1-4a; Psalm 121; Romans 4:1-5, 13-17; John 3:1-17 or Matthew 17:1-9

Invocation

We gather today in celebration of our birth into the kingdom of God.

Spirit of God, giver of new beginnings
Whose birthday gift to us is Love and Eternal Life,
Open our new eyes to see Love
High and lifted up, on the cross of Calvary.
Breathe into our new being the breath of life that lasts forever.
And reveal to us the kingdom of God in all its glory.

Benediction

Lift your eyes in confidence to our Maker.
Go forth in confidence under the Maker's watchful eye.
Our God, the Maker of heaven and earth, who watches
over your sleeping and your awakening,
your beginning and your ending,
Steps ahead of you, guarding your coming and going
Both now and forevermore.

Third Sunday in Lent

Lections: Exodus 17:1-7; Psalm 95; Romans 5:1-11; John
4:5-42

Invocation

God, I am no Moses, that I should strike a rock to yield its
sweet water for this spiritually thirsty people!
Nevertheless, I seek some sign of your presence, to still the
burning thirsty question: "Is the Lord with us or not?"
Then we hear the inviting words "Come, see a man . . . could
this be the Christ?"
Lord, you have been with your people through so much,
tried, tested, and true. So we quiet our questioning hearts and
clamoring voices. We bow down in worship before you, O
Lord our Maker.
And we know that we shall once again be well fed from your
gracious hand. Amen.

Benediction

Go now to express in your lives the beliefs that have been expressed here in word and song. No longer believe because of what has been said, but know for sure that this Jesus in whose name we have met is really the Savior of the world.

Fourth Sunday in Lent

Lections: 1 Samuel 16:1-13; Psalm 23; Ephesians 5:8-14; John 9:1-41

Invocation

Our Lord God,
Come as holy light to enlighten our minds.
Come as holy truth to teach us your way.
Come as holy wind to blow a fresh work of your Spirit.
Come as holy fire to cleanse us from all sin.
Come as holy power to send us into your service.

Benediction

"May God who gives patience, steadiness, and encouragement help you to live in complete harmony with each other—each with the attitude of Christ toward the other. And then all of us can praise the Lord together with one voice, giving glory to God, the Father of our Lord Jesus Christ" (Rom. 15:5, 6 TLB).

Fifth Sunday in Lent

Lections: Ezekiel 37:1-14; Psalm 130; Romans 8:6-11; John 11:1-45

Invocation

Eternal God,
You have come and revealed yourself to us
In your Son Jesus Christ.
You have sent your Spirit
To make Christ known to us.
And to indwell us.
We come this hour to set our minds on the things of the
Spirit,
To know the life and peace
Possible only through the quickening
Of your Spirit.
We open our hearts
To your regenerating work.

Benediction

Go forth from here strengthened by the Holy Spirit.
"If the Spirit of [the one] who raised Jesus from the dead
dwells in you, [the one] who raised Christ from the dead will
give life to your mortal bodies also through [God's] Spirit
that dwells in you" (Rom. 8:11).

Passion/Palm Sunday

Lections: Isaiah 50:4-9*a*; Psalm 118:1-2, 19-29; Philippians
2:5-11; Matthew 21:1-11

Invocation

O God, come among us.
We know something of the true way of blessedness
Revealed and realized in Christ.
We see his suffering and death—
The path of love that led to the cross,
The reward for faithfulness,

That led to the crown of thorns.
May we never be caught up in the momentum of hate.
Forgive when we have taken Christ's sacrifice lightly
Or failed to rejoice in our salvation.
May we share the Savior's sorrow for sin
And know the secret of his strength.
Help us see, even in the darkest hour of trial
The shining of the true light.

Benediction

Go forth from here; take up your cross.
Follow Christ in faith,
Knowing that he promised his presence
To all who faithfully follow in his footsteps.

Easter Season

Easter Day

Lections: Acts 10:34-43; Psalm 118:1-2, 14-24; Colossians 3:1-4; John 20:1-18

Invocation (based on Col. 3:1-4)

LEADER: All who come to this house of worship tell me what this day means to you.

PEOPLE: **Because Christ has been raised, we too**
(in unison) **have been raised with Christ who sits at the right hand of God. Therefore we will seek the things that are for our neighbor and set our minds on things other than ourselves. The old self has died and is now hidden with Christ in God. Christ is our life and when he comes again we will be with him.**

LEADER: Take your tambourines and enter into the joy of celebration, for death has been defeated.

Benediction (based on Ps. 118:22-24)

This is the day the Lord made.
We are glad for this opportunity to worship
a risen Lord.
The stone that the builders rejected has become the chief cornerstone.
This was the Lord's doing.
It is marvelous in our sight.
Send us forth as people of the Resurrection. Give us your strength. We beseech you.

Second Sunday of Easter

Lections: Acts 2:14*a*, 22-32; Psalm 16; 1 Peter 1:3-9; John 20:19-31

Invocation

In the name of the risen Christ, we gather for worship. We do not see God, and yet we believe enough to gather. We believe enough to worship. So may the unseen God be present in our midst. May the unseen Jesus fill us with the Holy Spirit. And with the eyes of faith, may we see God at work and rejoice. Amen.

Benediction

As God sent Jesus to be the light of the world, so now the Spirit of Jesus sends us out to the world around us. May God unlock the doors of our fears, that we might freely stand among the world's people, that we might share the touch of Jesus, that we might speak his words, "Peace be with you."

Third Sunday of Easter

Lections: Acts 2:14*a*, 36-41; Psalm 116:1-4, 12-19; 1 Peter 1:17-23; Luke 24:13-35

Invocation

Come among us, O God,
For you have ransomed us from our futile ways,
Not with the perishable things
Such as silver or gold,
But with the precious blood of Christ.
And it is through him
That we have come to love you
And to trust you.

We have come to set our faith and hope in you.
Make all of these
Greater realities, we pray,
As we meet and worship today.

Benediction

Go forth from here in the great assurance of the scripture, "Blessed be the God and Father of our Lord Jesus Christ, which according to his abundant mercy hath begotten us again unto a lively hope by the resurrection of Jesus Christ from the dead, to an inheritance incorruptible, and undefiled, and that fadeth not away, reserved in heaven for you" (1 Pet. 1:3-4 KJV).

Fourth Sunday of Easter

Lections: Acts 2:42-47; Psalm 23; 1 Peter 2:19-25; John 10:1-10

Invocation

O great Shepherd of the earth, come to us in this place of worship. Even when we resist, come to us with your support and reckless love. Come to us, revealing your Son our Savior afresh. Come to us in the power and presence of your Holy Spirit.

Benediction

As you leave here today, leave with glad hearts and generous minds. Leave with Christ's teaching within your spirit so that you may minister to those without love and without hope. In the name of Jesus Christ our Lord. Amen.

Fifth Sunday of Easter

Lections: Acts 7:55-60; Psalm 31:1-5, 15-16; 1 Peter 2:2-10; John 14:1-14

Invocation

Come, Risen Christ among us.
We long to know your will
And to grow in your likeness.
You call us your spiritual house
In which you dwell,
Your holy priesthood,
Through whom you minister.
Help us to offer spiritual sacrifices,
Acceptable unto you, O God,
Through our Lord Jesus Christ.
Give us a vision of all those things also,
Which you are even now preparing for us.

Benediction

Go from here, as God's chosen race,
As God's royal priesthood, as God's holy nation
As God's very own people.
Go, proclaiming the mighty acts of him who called you
Out of darkness
Into his marvelous light, who gave new hope
For life here and hereafter.

Sixth Sunday of Easter

Lections: Acts 17:22-31; Psalm 66:8-20; 1 Peter 3:13-22; John 14:15-21

Invocation

O God, O Christ, O Holy Spirit,
You have promised your abiding presence
Among your people.
Lord Jesus, you have said,
Where two or three are gathered in your name,
You will be there.
Holy Spirit, intercede in our behalf.
We claim your presence.
Open our hearts and minds to receive
All you desire to give, as we unite in your presence now.

Benediction

"Now may our Lord Jesus Christ . . . and God . . . who loved
us and through grace gave us eternal comfort and good hope,
comfort your hearts and strengthen them in every good work
and word" (2 Thess. 2:16, 17).

Seventh Sunday of Easter

Lections: Acts 1:6-14; Psalm 68:1-10, 32-35; 1 Peter 4:12-14;
5:6-11; John 17:1-11

Invocation

We've come from what seems like a whirlwind of activities
and overloaded schedules. Now we're sitting in this place of
worship hoping to be stilled. Our minds are still cluttered by
the things we've been doing and by what we have yet to do.
Our thoughts and emotions are inattentive because of strug-
gling relationships and unsettling circumstances.
May we instead get caught up in the hope of comfort. May
our thoughts be dominated by words that bring peace. May
our emotions be calmed by your Spirit.

O Christ, help us to concentrate on you, your Word, and your Holy Spirit, that we may worship you in Spirit and in truth.

Benediction

Lord God, as you told your disciples that they would receive power to be witnesses, may we also be sent forth with power to witness concerning you.

When we encounter discord and injustice, may we give witness to your peace. When we encounter poverty and brokenness, may we give witness to your compassion. When we come across pain and suffering, may we give witness to your healing and comfort. When we come across spiritual deprivation, may we give witness to your salvation.

We ask that we would be able both to accept the trials of life, and do all that we can to alleviate them, recognizing that in you Lord, we live and move and have our being.

Season After Pentecost

Trinity Sunday
(First Sunday After Pentecost)

Lections: Genesis 1:1–2:4*a*; Psalm 8; 2 Corinthians 13:11-13; Matthew 28:16-20

Invocation

Sovereign Creator of earth and sky,
Savior always with us,
Spirit sweeping over the waters,
   renew our hearts today,
   surround us with grace,
   fill us with wonder and awe,
      so we may honor you
      with our gifts of love and praise
      and worship you with our whole life.

Benediction

May the love of God,
   the grace of the Lord Jesus Christ
   and the communion of the Holy Spirit
      be with you all
      now and forever (based on 2 Cor. 13:11-13).

Sunday Between May 29 and June 4
Inclusive (if after Trinity Sunday)

Lections: Genesis 6:9-22; 7:24; 8:14-19; Psalm 46; Romans 1:16-17; 3:22*b*-28, (29-31); Matthew 7:21-29

Invocation

O Lord our Savior,
Our God and Creator,

We kneel in our need
That we might arise in your strength.
We come into your presence
That we might go forth in your power.
We come to worship
That we might go as your unashamed witnesses.
We desire your touch in our lives
So that we may touch
With your love, everyone we meet.

Benediction

As you go from here
I ask that "Our God will make you worthy of his call and will fulfill by his power every good resolve and work of faith, so that the name of our Lord Jesus may be glorified in you, and you in him, according to the grace of our God and the Lord Jesus Christ" (2 Thess. 1:11-12).

Sunday Between June 5 and June 11 Inclusive (if after Trinity Sunday)

Lections: Genesis 12:1-9; Psalm 33:1-12; Romans 4:13-25; Matthew 9:9-13, 18-26

Invocation

O Lord, you have called us to follow you.
Grant us the grace,
like Abram, to hope in your promises;
like Matthew, to put you before our work;
like the girl raised to life, to renew our own lives;
like the woman healed, to believe you will heal us.
This day, we come to you again, Lord,
to better learn how to follow you.
Lead us.

Benediction

God be with you as you continue to follow
the one who called Abram;
the one who called Matthew;
the one who recalled the girl to life; and
the woman to health.
You, too, are called.
Live this week in the warmth of being wanted,
and in the strength of God's help.

Sunday Between June 12 and June 18 Inclusive (if after Trinity Sunday)

Lections: Genesis 18:1-15, (21:1-7); Psalm 116:1-2, 12-19; Romans 5:1-8; Matthew 9:35–10:8, (9-23)

Invocation

O Lord, we need a drink of water, and something to eat,
here, now, in the shade during the heat of the day.
We need your ear, too, while we rest at your gracious table.

Will you listen to our journey's tale—of how short our
life is,
and of our disappointments, and of the many times we
got lost,
and of our surprise that we have arrived this far?
Your sanctuary, Lord, is an oasis for us weary travelers.

Benediction

Thank you, Lord, for mercifully listening this morning.
Your silence has given us space to remember
the cup of your salvation,
the many times you surprised us with new birth and
youthful energy.

We feel restored to our best selves.
Instead of trudging along, we can go now,
with new strength, and a more hopeful faith.
With your refreshment so freely given,
we return to our lives with new perspective.
Thank you, Lord.

Sunday Between June 19 and June 25 Inclusive (if after Trinity Sunday)

Lections: Genesis 21:8-21; Psalm 86:1-10, 16-17; Romans 6:1*b*-11; Matthew 10:24-39

Invocation

O God, our heavenly Creator, we thank you for your Word and for those eternal truths that guide us day by day. We thank you for the Living Word, our Lord and Savior Jesus Christ, and for the deep assurance that he is here, present with us. Teach us, in our time together, to turn unto you so your thoughts may be our thoughts and your ways may become our ways.

Benediction

As you go from here know that
"God is able to provide you with every blessing in abundance, so that you may always have enough of everything and may provide in abundance for every good work" (2 Cor. 9:8 RSV).

Sunday Between June 26 and July 2 Inclusive

Lections: Genesis 22:1-14; Psalm 13; Romans 6:12-23; Matthew 10:40-42

Invocation

We have come this morning to Mount Moriah, Lord
Here we are with the things we treasure
At the altar of sacrifice.
We've come, Lord, fearful of letting them go.
Here at the storehouse of your riches in glory,
Here, Lord, this morning on Mount Moriah, be our
Provider.
Set us free from our fears
And open our hearts to your treasures of
Grace
Holiness
And eternal Life. Amen.

Benediction

We have seen your glory on this mountain, Lord.
The demands of your holiness have shaken us
And drawn us to your unfailing love.

As we leave this mountain, give light to our eyes.
Put a song of praise for your great love on our lips
And direct our steps to walk in your ways.

Sunday Between July 3 and July 9 Inclusive

Lections: Genesis 24:34-38, 42-49, 58-67; Psalm 45:10-17 or
Song of Solomon 2:8-13; Romans 7:15-25*a*; Matthew 11:16-19,
25-30

Invocation

Come, gracious God, we enter this place out of a broken,
hurting, and often violent world.
—Where we lay blame, you O Lord are gracious and full of
compassion.

—When we respond in anger, you O Lord are slow to anger and rich in love.

—When we rely on weapons of war, you O Lord come gentle and riding on a donkey.

—When we despoil the earth with our greedy consumption, you O Lord have
compassion on all you have made.

When the world we experience is too much for us, your love is greatest. Thank you for inviting us into your gracious presence. We pray in the name of Christ, the Prince of Peace. Amen.

Benediction

Go into the world, all you who are weary and burdened, having experienced for this short hour the rest that comes in the presence of Christ. May you go now, refreshed and encouraged, to seek his will, and do the work of the one who said, "Take my yoke upon you and learn from me."

Sunday Between July 10 and July 16 Inclusive

Lections: Genesis 25:19-34; Psalm 119:105-112; Romans 8:1-11; Matthew 13:1-9, 18-23

Invocation

Come among us, O God,
To give us ears that do not fail to hear,
To give us eyes that do not fail to see,
To give us hearts that do not fail to respond.
Make us soil,
Which receives the seeds of truth
To bear fruit abundant.

Benediction

Go from here with God's blessing
"And God is able to make all grace abound toward you; that ye, always having all sufficiency in all things, may abound to every good work" (2 Cor. 9:8 KJV).

Sunday Between July 17 and July 23 Inclusive

Lections: Genesis 28:10-19*a*; Psalm 139:1-12, 23-24; Romans 8:12-25; Matthew 13:24-30, 36-43

Invocation

Eternal and Almighty God, we come into your presence this day seeking your mercy and grace. We gather in wonder and praise to worship you with pure intent. Our daily lives reflect both light and darkness, confidence and fear, joy and sadness; thus, we seek your love and care. Quiet our lives before you as we worship. We praise you that we are heirs of your grace and children led by your Spirit. Remove from us anything that would dull our alertness to your presence and promptings as we worship in the name of your Son, Jesus. Amen.

Benediction

May God's grace and mercy follow you wherever you go and whatever you do. May Jesus' teachings and redeeming love give you a disciplined, holy life. May the Holy Spirit's presence give you joy in serving others and being a light in this world's darkness. Go in peace. Amen.

Sunday Between July 24 and July 30 Inclusive

Lections: Genesis 29:15-28; Psalm 105:1-11, 45*b* or Psalm 128; Romans 8:26-39; Matthew 13:31-33, 44-52

Invocation

God of the ages, God of a thousand generations
Thank you for giving us this lifetime.
We remember that you covenanted with our ancestors.
We remember that you believed in us before we believed
in you.
Lord stand among us
blessing us and keeping us.
As we seek your face,
reveal yourself to us in this service. Amen.

Benediction

Go from this place in humble adoration of the one
whose place
Is the timelessness of space
And whose existence is expressed
"I was. I am. I shall be."
Go from this place in adoration of Christ
who left that glorious realm with fervent love
personally for you and personally for me!
Go from this place in confidence.
Nothing can ever separate us from that Love! Amen.

Sunday Between July 31 and August 6 Inclusive

Lections: Genesis 32:22-31; Psalm 17:1-7, 15; Romans 9:1-5; Matthew 14:13-21

Invocation

Come among us, our God
We would hear your call to us—
Come all you who are thirsty,
come to the waters.
And you who have no money,
come, rest awhile!
Come all who wrestled with God,
as did Jacob at Peniel.
And you who are in need of blessing,
give ear and come.
Hear, that your soul may live.
Come let us worship the Lord.
Everyone come! Welcome to the house of the Lord.

Benediction

I have made an everlasting covenant with you;
my faithful love.
The same covenant as promised to your ancestors.
Therefore, as you leave this place know that you take God's promise of faithful love. God will hear your prayer. Go in peace.

Sunday Between August 7 and August 13 Inclusive

Lections: Genesis 37:1-4, 12-28; Psalm 105:1-6, 16-22, 45*b*; Romans 10:5-15; Matthew 14:22-33

Invocation

We praise you Lord God. We praise you because you are our God and the redeemer of your people. You provide for our needs and you give us blessings. We praise you because you speak to us when we gather before you. May we commune

with you in our prayers. May our spirits be lifted as we worship you in song. May our wills be strengthened and our direction be clarified as we meditate upon your Word.
We confess you as Lord. And we lift our hearts to worship you. Amen.

Benediction

We praise you again Lord for this time of worship together. We've listened for the quiet nudging of your Spirit. We've sought the stirrings of your movings. We want to respond to your calling to us.
Help us to take courage and to not be afraid as we step out in faith to the things you'll ask from us this week. May each thought and deed be guided by your Spirit. May our motives and intentions be influenced by the principles taught in your Word. May our desire be to live so as to honor and glorify your name O Lord.
We go with your peace. We go with your love. We go with your hope. Amen.

Sunday Between August 14 and August 20 Inclusive

Lections: Genesis 45:1-15; Psalm 133; Romans 11:1-2*a*, 29-32; Matthew 15:(10-20), 21-28

Invocation

Our God
We meet in your name and presence.
We invite you among us.
We claim your promise to meet with all those who call upon you.
Because we meet together today
May life be enlarged for those who lack hope,

May life be clarified for those confused,
May life be sweeter for those who taste the bitterness of it,
May life be holy for those who may have lost
the dignity, beauty, and meaning of it.

Benediction

As you go "I want to remind you that your strength must
come from the Lord's mighty power within you. Put on all
of God's armor so that you will be able to stand safe against
all strategies and tricks of Satan" (Eph. 6:10-11 TLB).

Sunday Between August 21 and August 27 Inclusive

Lections: Exodus 1:8–2:10; Psalm 124; Romans 12:1-8;
Matthew 16:13-20

Invocation

O Lord, we give you this hour,
to show our thanks and sing your praise.
We give you our work,
knowing that you will fulfill your purposes.
We give you our time,
asking you to guide us in what is good and acceptable and
perfect.
We give you our friends and families,
seeking to follow your example of how to love and bless
them.
We give you our lives,
trusting that you will not forsake the work of your hands.
All that we are and all that we have, is yours. Receive it to
your glory and praise, through Jesus Christ our Lord. Amen.

Benediction

Receive back your time, your work, your friends, your family, and your lives. For as you have submitted it to God for ownership and blessing, God, in turn, seeks your partnership in using all that you are and have in the days ahead. Go in the joy and peace of life in Jesus Christ. Amen.

Sunday Between August 28 and September 3 Inclusive

Lections: Exodus 3:1-15; Psalm 105:1-6, 23-26, 45*c*; Romans 12:9-21; Matthew 16:21-28

Invocation

Come among us once again for we have come to hear your Word and your wonderful works. We have come to see and hear the living Word, Christ himself. Teach us this day to hear with humble ears. Set our minds this hour on divine things.

Benediction

We leave here today as Christ's committed ones, holding on to the good, loving our brothers and sisters, feeding our enemy. We need you to go with us O Lord, for this is a commitment larger than our own grace or grit. Travel with us in the steadiness of your embracing presence and in the strength of your enabling power. We pray through Jesus Christ, our Lord. Amen.

Sunday Between September 4 and September 10 Inclusive

Lections: Exodus 12:1-14; Psalm 149; Romans 13:8-14; Matthew 18:15-20

Invocation

O God, Creator and Redeemer,
Reveal yourself and your will.
We come, united in worship as your people.
We come, dependent upon your grace, which gives us so much more of your love than we deserve.
We come, dependent upon your mercy, which withholds the just judgment we do deserve.
We come, dependent upon your forgiveness, which removes our guilt and remembers our sin no more.
We come, desiring to know you better and to take on your likeness in all our relationships and responsibilities.

Benediction

"May the Lord bring you into an ever deeper understanding of the love of God and of the patience that comes from Christ" (2 Thess. 3:5 TLB).

Sunday Between September 11 and September 17 Inclusive

Lections: Exodus 14:19-31; Psalm 114 or Exodus 15:1b-11, 20-21; Romans 14:1-12; Matthew 18:21-35

Invocation

Our God, we long to sense your presence.
It's been a rough week, Lord.

Our backs have been against the wall
with no way to escape.
In our desperation we remember your goodness to Israel
at the Red Sea.
Make an escape for us through our wall,
All the way into your sanctuary.
And when we are in, Lord,
Shut the door on our pursuers.
Grant us safety. Grant us peace. Grant us joy.
For this we praise you. For this we exalt you. Amen.

Benediction

Go from this place praising God.
For God has gained the VICTORY!
God has provided an escape from our enemies.
Go forth healed! Go forth forgiven! Go forth redeemed! Go
forth crowned and satisfied!
And as God has treated you, so treat one another. Amen.

Sunday Between September 18 and September 24 Inclusive

Lections: Exodus 16:2-15; Psalm 105:1-6, 37-45; Philippians
1:21-30; Matthew 20:1-16

Invocation

Lord, we gather this morning—your children
Blessed Free Wealthy Comfortable Yours
You have gathered us from
Anger Pain Bondage Grumbling Disappointments
Disease
Teach us contentment and gratefulness
Hearts that remember deliverance
Bodies healthfully sustained

Minds stretched by remembering
Continue to remind us of your grace to us,
Your loving care of your people.
Meet with us. Cause us to remember.

Benediction

I commend you to God
who is able to see you through all the situations of life
that you will face this week.
Open your life to Jesus for his caring and companionship.
May his blessing follow you and the Holy Spirit guide you.
Amen.

Sunday Between September 25 and October 1 Inclusive

Lections: Exodus 17:1-7; Psalm 78:1-4, 12-16; Philippians 2:1-13; Matthew 21:23-32

Invocation

Our Lord and God, we come together by your love, mercy, and grace. We confess we can be cast down and disquieted so easily as we wander in the spiritual wilderness of our workaday world. We need the consciousness and encouragement of your presence. Reveal to us anew how much we can receive when we enter your house, in your presence and in the presence of others whom you love. Renew the eternal prospective we need to keep faithful to Christ in the day-by-day relationships and decisions of life, in our time together.

Benediction

Now go from here as God's own family, children beloved by God. And live in the likeness of God's Son Jesus Christ in the power of his Spirit as you go.

May the grace, mercy, and peace of our Lord our God rest upon you, day by day, and moment by moment, by God's Spirit, who dwells in you.

Sunday Between October 2 and October 8 Inclusive

Lections: Exodus 20:1-4, 7-9, 12-20; Psalm 19; Philippians 3:4b-14; Matthew 21:33-46

Invocation

O God, as we come together for worship, we move from the mundane that is so much a part of our lives, to take time to think again of those things that are eternal—for truth and love, for joy and peace, for hope and holiness. And, today may we see again that you bring yourself and all that is eternal into the most mundane experiences of life as we recognize you as our God and Savior. Show us yourself and meet our needs this hour.

Benediction

"Now to [God] who is able to keep you from falling, and to make you stand without blemish in the presence of [God's] glory with rejoicing, to the only God our Savior, through Jesus Christ our Lord, be glory, majesty, power, and authority, before all time and now and forever" (Jude 24-25).

Sunday Between October 9 and October 15 Inclusive

Lections: Exodus 32:1-14; Psalm 106:1-6, 19-23; Philippians 4:1-9; Matthew 22:1-14

Invocation

Almighty God, fountain of all good, kindle in us insight and inspiration in our time together so that this hour may have significance for time and eternity. Open our ears that we may hear your voice. Soften our hearts to receive your truth. Reveal yourself to us that we may learn to find you everywhere. May we become unobstructed channels of your love and of your saving grace and goodness.

Benediction

Leave here today knowing that
"It is in God's power to provide you richly with every good gift; thus you will have ample means in yourselves to meet each and every situation, with enough and to spare for every good cause" (2 Cor. 9:8 NEB).

Sunday Between October 16 and October 22 Inclusive

Lections: Exodus 33:12-23; Psalm 99; 1 Thessalonians 1:1-10; Matthew 22:15-22

Invocation

LEADER: The Lord reigns, let the nations beware;
            the Lord sits between heavenly hosts,
            let the earth shake. Great is the Lord,
            exalted over all the nations. Let us praise
            the Lord's great and awesome name.
            The Lord is holy!

PEOPLE: **The Lord is mighty and loves justice.**
            Equity has been established: in Jacob the
            Lord has done what is just and right. Exalt
            the Lord and worship at God's footstool.
            The Lord is holy!

LEADER: Moses and Aaron were among the priests, Samuel was among those God called. They called on the Lord and the Lord answered them. The Lord spoke to them from a pillar of cloud. They kept statutes and decrees the Lord gave them. The Lord is holy!

PEOPLE: **O Lord our God, as you answered them, answer us; as you forgave Israel, forgive us; as you invited them to worship, enter our worship, You are a holy God!**

Benediction

LEADER: Remember what the Lord says to the assembled.

PEOPLE: **I will go before you and will level mountains; I will break down gates of bronze and cut through gates of iron. I will give you treasures of darkness, riches stored in secret places. I call on you by name and bestow on you a title of honor.**

LEADER: There is no other Lord, there is no other God from the rising of the sun to the place of its setting. Remind others there is none besides the Lord.

Sunday Between October 23 and October 29 Inclusive

Lections: Deuteronomy 34:1-12; Psalm 90:1-6, 13-17; 1 Thessalonians 2:1-8; Matthew 22:34-46

Invocation

Lord, you have been our dwelling place in all generations. So now in this generation, so now on this day,

Dwell among us, as we gather together in the name of our
Lord Jesus.
You are God, we are mortals;
you are from everlasting to everlasting.
We are like grass; we flourish and wither in your sight.
Satisfy us this morning with your steadfast love,
so that we may rejoice and be glad all our days.
Grant us the vision to see with eyes of faith,
to see as Moses did into the land of promise,
the things you will yet do in our lives, in our homes and in
our church.
Our hope is in you. Amen.

Benediction

May the God who is now, and always will be, go with you.
May you be aware of God working within your world this
week,
through the love that has been created in your heart and soul
and mind.
May you know God's glorious power alive among the children of God.
And may the favor of the Lord our God be upon you, and
prosper the work of your hands. Amen.

Sunday Between October 30 and November 5 Inclusive

Lections: Joshua 3:7-17; Psalm 107:1-7, 33-37; 1 Thessalonians
2:9-13; Matthew 23:1-12

Invocation

O God, today we thank you for all those in whose words
truth comes to us, for all who in every generation have taught
and explained and preached the Word of truth, the Scripture.

May we never listen to any teaching that would minimize the seriousness of sin or make virtue less important. Give us minds quick to discern truth and error. Give us hearts quick to follow your revealed will. Give us such love for you and your will that the false may not lure us and we might love and live your truth, through Jesus Christ our Lord.

Benediction

As you go I pray that you may know God's power in practice. "I pray that out of the glorious richness of [God's] resources [God] will enable you to know the strength of the Spirit's inner re-inforcement—that Christ may actually live in your hearts by your faith. And I pray that you, rooted and founded in love yourselves, may be able to grasp (with all Christians), how wide and long and deep and high is the love of Christ— and to know for yourselves that love so far above our understanding. So will you be filled through all your being with God" (Eph. 3:16-19 JBP).

Sunday Between November 6 and November 12 Inclusive

Lections: Joshua 24:1-3*a*, 14-25; Psalm 78:1-7; 1 Thessalonians 4:13-18; Matthew 25:1-13

Invocation

Let us set our hope in God,
and the works of God!
Let us incline our ears to the teachings of God,
to what we have heard and known.
Let us renew our covenant with God,
and hold the name of God before all our interactions.
Let us teach what we know of God,
so that our children will set their hope in God.
Let us attend to our lights,

for behold, the bridegroom is here!
Amen.

Benediction

We have listened to the Word of God.
We have renewed our hope in God.
We have remembered our covenant with God.
Go forth, into the week, now,
in the light of God's grace and love.
Amen.

Sunday Between November 13 and November 19 Inclusive

Lections: Judges 4:1-7; Psalm 123; 1 Thessalonians 5:1-11; Matthew 25:14-30

Invocation

Lord, you have been our dwelling place in all generations.
Before the mountains were brought forth,
or ever you had formed the earth and the world,
From everlasting to everlasting, you are God.
(Silence)
We stand before you in fear, considering the power of your wrath, the force of your anger.
Have mercy on us, O Lord.
Our days are numbered. Some are many, others just a few.
Teach us to count our days that we may be wise.
Have mercy on us, O Lord our God,
For you have been our dwelling place in all generations.
Amen.

Benediction

Children of light, children of the day—

Take heart encouraging one another.
Put on faith, hope, and love,
For God has destined us not for wrath,
But for obtaining salvation through our Lord Jesus Christ,
who died for us,
So that whether we are awake or asleep we may live with
him. Amen.

Reign of Christ/Christ the King Sunday

Lections: Ezekiel 34:11-16, 20-24; Psalm 100; Ephesians
1:15-23; Matthew 25:31-46

Invocation

O Christ,
Before whom all nations shall finally bow,
Before whom all rulers will cast their crowns,
Before whom all creatures shall acknowledge your rule,
Cause us to bow in adoration,
Cause us to cast all before you,
Cause us to acknowledge your Lordship,
Now in this time together,
Now and when we separate,
Now and each day and hour.

Benediction

Go from this place
As those acknowledging Christ's Kingship
Leave this place
As those who live under his Lordship,
In your homes, businesses, and pleasure,
From this day forward.

Year B

Advent Season

First Sunday of Advent

Lections: Isaiah 64:1-9; Psalm 80:1-7, 17-19; 1 Corinthians 1:3-9; Mark 13:24-37

Invocation

Today, O God,
We are united together in your presence,
In the fellowship of your Son, Jesus.
And though we come from many different places
And come with many different needs,
We know that you will pour out your blessing
So that, as we leave,
We may leave with the consciousness
That we have met you today.
For this we praise you.

Benediction

As you go
Know that Christ goes with you.
Know the bond of fellowship you have in Christ.
Know the communion of the Holy Spirit.
Know that God's Word is truth. And it shall not pass away.

Second Sunday of Advent

Lections: Isaiah 40:1-11; Psalm 85:1-2, 8-13; 2 Peter 3:8-15a; Mark 1:1-8

Invocation

We know, O God, we need to come to you.
We invite you to come to us.

You created us for your glory and service.
And we confess that we have sinned,
In thought, word, and deed.
Teach us true repentance.
In the multitude of your mercies
And the largeness of your steadfast love
Forgive our sins.
Mold our hearts and wills
To love and serve you more perfectly.

Benediction

"May the God of peace . . . sanctify you entirely; and may your spirit and soul and body be kept sound and blameless at the coming of our Lord Jesus Christ. The one who calls you is faithful, and . . . will do this" (1 Thess. 5:23-24).

Third Sunday of Advent

Lections: Isaiah 61:1-4, 8-11; Psalm 126 or Luke 1:47-55; 1 Thessalonians 5:16-24; John 1:6-8, 19-28

Invocation

Come into this gathering today, Lord
binding up our brokenheartedness, freeing us from our shackles,
releasing us from our blindness, and replacing our sadness with joy.
Take off our garment of despair, Lord.
And dress us with party clothes of praise!
Come to us Lord Jesus
adorn us with Hope;
adorn us with Gladness;
adorn us with Praise. Amen.

Benediction

We came this morning cold; Lord, you warmed us.
We came this morning poor; Lord, you enriched us.
We came this morning hungry; Lord, you filled us.
We came this morning undeserving; Lord, you showed us
mercy.
Now, Lord, as we go,
may your fullness and your mercy flow through us
filling the hungry and warming the hopeless.
Go from this place warmed by the Spirit's fire! Amen.

Fourth Sunday of Advent

Lections: 2 Samuel 7:1-11, 16; Luke 1:47-55 or Psalm 89:1-4,
19-26; Romans 16:25-27; Luke 1:26-38

Invocation

Lord God
Your mercies are new every morning
And your mercy is for those who reverence you
From generation to generation.
Today we thank you that your mercy
Has come, even to us today,
Shown in the sending of your Son,
Our Savior Jesus Christ, the Lord.
Today may we see your full salvation.
May we know your compassions, which do not fail.
May we be freed from every bondage
Through the indwelling Christ.

Benediction

Go forth in the name of Jesus.
Do justly, love mercy,
And walk humbly with your God.

Christmas Season

First Sunday After Christmas Day

Lections: Isaiah 61:10–62:3; Psalm 148; Galatians 4:4-7; Luke 2:22-40

Invocation

Praise the Lord!
Our whole being exults in you, O God,
because we have seen the Messiah!
We have reenacted, once again,
the Christ Child being born into this world
to make a difference in our lives.
We have received the gift of Jesus' life
and we gather to praise you.
In the name of Jesus,
Amen.

Benediction

You are a crown of beauty in the hand of the Lord,
and a band of jewels in the heart of your God.

You are clothed in the garments of salvation
and in robes of righteousness.

Therefore, let joy and praise fill your heart and soul
to overflowing. Praise the Lord!

Second Sunday After Christmas Day

Lections: Jeremiah 31:7-14; Psalm 147:12-20; Ephesians 1:3-14; John 1:(1-9), 10-18

Invocation

Father, we come to worship with the songs of Christmas still in our ears. We celebrate today the joy that the wise men found when they came to celebrate the birth of Jesus. We come as they did to worship and praise the Savior. There was anxiety and anticipation as they traveled those many miles, just as we come today with our anxiety and anticipation as we search for the truth and life found only in Jesus. Help us, as we worship to see and to follow the light of your Son, and then may we go with joy proclaiming, "Jesus Christ is born."

Benediction

As we go from here, our Creator, help us to go with faces brightened by peace and joy that is found only in you. Help us light the path so that others may see and come to know the Christ we love and adore; the Christ we serve and the Christ who sends us forth as his faithful followers.

Season After the Epiphany

....

Baptism of the Lord
(First Sunday After the Epiphany)

Lections: Genesis 1:1-5; Psalm 29; Acts 19:1-7; Mark 1:4-11

Invocation

God, your voice broke through the silence of our night
this morning with a clarion call.
God, what a beautiful morning!
God, what a beautiful day!
Your voice is powerful; your voice is majestic.
It pierces the darkness of our night and calls us to praise!
Thank you for waking us.
God, what a beautiful morning!
God, what a beautiful day! Amen.

Benediction

Bless us, O God, with the presence of your Holy Spirit
hovering over the deep waters of our journey,
wrapping us with light, scattering our night with day!
Don't abandon us to our own chaos—spiritless, formless,
and empty.
Bless us, O God, with the presence of your creating Spirit,
filling our empty hearts with love, bringing sunrise to our
troubled night.
Let there be morning
Let there be day. Amen.

Second Sunday After the Epiphany

Lections: 1 Samuel 3:1-10, (11-20); Psalm 139:1-6, 13-18;
1 Corinthians 6:12-20; John 1:43-51

Invocation

In the busyness of each day, in the stillness of this moment, God is ever present. In our homes and in our workplaces, in our schools and in our neighborhoods, at work and at worship, God calls us by name. God calls us to follow Jesus. God calls us to holy living. May our ears be open to hear God's Word. May our minds and bodies be ready to respond. Speak, Lord, for your servants are listening.

Benediction

Here we are Lord. Like the young Samuel ministering in the temple, we are ready to serve. Like Jesus' first disciples, we are ready to follow. Like the early church, we are ready to glorify God. Here we are, Lord. We have heard your call. Now with the presence of Jesus and by the power of the Holy Spirit, may we carry that call into your world. Amen.

Third Sunday After the Epiphany

Lections: Jonah 3:1-5, 10; Psalm 62:5-12; 1 Corinthians 7:29-31; Mark 1:14-20

Invocation

Eternal God, our Creator, Sustainer, Redeemer,
You are ever coming to us
And from you we are ever turning.
Forgive our wandering ways.
Come among us as we gather.
Help us draw near in true repentance with full assurance of faith
Until we see afresh in Jesus Christ,
Until we hear, with the heart, your Word of truth,
Until we pray in confidence through the Holy Spirit,

Until we worship you in Spirit and in truth,
With joy and rejoicing, Through Jesus Christ, our Lord.

Benediction

You came to worship together;
Go now to serve.
You have been given light;
Go now to let it shine.
You have been blessed with God's love;
Go now to share that love. You are Christ's disciples.
Go now to witness to all, in Christ's name.

Fourth Sunday After the Epiphany

Lections: Deuteronomy 18:15-20; Psalm 111; 1 Corinthians 8:1-13; Mark 1:21-28

Invocation

O God, as we gather today we thank you for the faith of those who, over the centuries, have passed on the faith. We know we are here today by your grace and also because of the faithfulness of those who have gone before us. May we also transmit the faith in unsullied and undimmed witness so that those who follow may come to know you and your will. Fortify us with true faith as we draw inspiration and incentive to be faithful in our time.

Benediction

"May the God of steadfastness and encouragement grant you to live in harmony with one another, in accordance with Christ Jesus, so that together you may with one voice glorify the God and Father of our Lord Jesus Christ" (Rom. 15:5-6).

Fifth Sunday After the Epiphany

Lections: Isaiah 40:21-31; Psalm 147:1-11, 20*c*; 1 Corinthians 9:16-23; Mark 1:29-39

Invocation

Our kind heavenly Creator,
We long for your presence.
And we humbly seek your face. We approach your throne
Through the merits of your Son, our Savior.
Thank you that your throne is a throne of grace.
We confess our sins of commission and omission.
Come with your healing presence.
And, according to your promise,
We receive your unmerited favor and forgiveness.
Through Jesus Christ, our Lord.

Benediction

As you have come into Christ's healing presence,
Go forth to heal, to bless, to serve
In the name of Jesus.
Live in the grace of the Lord Jesus.

Sixth Sunday After the Epiphany

Lections: 2 Kings 5:1-14; Psalm 30; 1 Corinthians 9:24-27; Mark 1:40-45

Invocation

We invoke your presence here, O God,
For it is out of our darkness
That we seek your light.
It is out of our sorrow
That we seek your joy.
It is out of our doubts
That we seek your certainty.

It is out of our restlessness
That we seek your peace.
It is out of our sin
That we seek your forgiveness.
Satisfy us early. We ask you through Christ.

Benediction

"Now may the Lord of peace personally give you peace at all times and in all ways. The Lord be with you all" (2 Thess. 3:16 JBP).

Seventh Sunday After the Epiphany

Lections: Isaiah 43:18-25; Psalm 41; 2 Corinthians 1:18-22; Mark 2:1-12

Invocation

O Lord, you are the one who breaks into our lives with new things. You make a way for us in the midst of a barren desert. You give drink to a thirsty people. You deliver us from trouble. You blot out our transgressions for the sake of your holy name. You heal us from our infirmities.
Gracious God, we welcome your presence into our lives this day. Be to us all that you desire, that we may worship you in Spirit and in truth. Amen.

Benediction

Blessed be the Lord, the God of Israel, from everlasting to everlasting. You have formed us for yourself, that we might declare your praise.
May our faithful God, whose promises are fulfilled in Jesus Christ, be with you as you leave this place. Amen.

Eighth Sunday After the Epiphany

Lections: Hosea 2:14-20; Psalm 103:1-13, 22; 2 Corinthians 3:1-6; Mark 2:13-22

Invocation

Eternal and ever blessed God,
You have called us by your grace.
We wait upon you.
We are dependent upon you.
Without your blessing we are restless.
Without your care we cannot live.
Without your love we cannot be saved.
Make our worship such today that
Every evil thought may be banished,
Every wandering thought may be arraigned,
And every imagination may be brought into captivity,
To the obedience of Jesus Christ.

Benediction

As Christ has called you to follow him
So he sends you forth.
Go, as his true disciples.
Go, and Christ will go with you.

Ninth Sunday After the Epiphany

Lections: Deuteronomy 5:12-15; Psalm 81:1-10; 2 Corinthians 4:5-12; Mark 2:23–3:6

Invocation

O God, we gather again by your mercy, and we seek to give you glory and praise. We praise you that you are the God of all grace and forgiveness. We want to take on your likeness that the life of the Lord Jesus might be made visible in our bodies. You are the giver of all the blessings of this present

67

life and our hope of life everlasting. May these moments together be a reminder of your love and make us grateful for all your goodness.

Benediction

As you depart from this place of worship,
Go in the consciousness of Christ's presence within you,
Through the Holy Spirit.
Go, with the consciousness
That the life of the Lord Jesus
Is made visible through you.

Last Sunday After the Epiphany (Transfiguration Sunday)

Lections: 2 Kings 2:1-12; 2 Corinthians 4:3-6; Psalm 50:1-6; Mark 9:2-9

Invocation

Lord God,
You have made manifest your glory and power
In the gospel of your Son, our Savior.
Reveal Christ again in this time of worship.
We desire pure hearts, so that we might see you.
We desire sincere love, so that we might trust you.
We desire sincere joy, so that we might praise you.
How very much we need you, O God,
In this time of worship.

Benediction

May the love and grace of Christ
Be so real to each of you
That those who meet you
This coming week
May know the real and living Christ.

Lenten Season

....

First Sunday in Lent

Lections: Genesis 9:8-17; Psalm 25:1-10; 1 Peter 3:18-22; Mark 1:9-15

Invocation

O God, today, in this hour of united worship,
Turn our hearts toward you.
Touch our spirits by your Spirit.
Teach us your everlasting truth.
Come with conviction and revelation.
That we may be convicted of our wrong
And that you may reveal your forgiveness
And your desire for our lives.
Transform our lives into the likeness of your Son, our Savior and Lord.
For it is in his name we ask it all. Amen.

Benediction

And now, as God's dear children, through the adoption into God's family, by Jesus Christ, go forth. Be strong in the Lord and the power of his boundless resource. Put on God's complete armor so that you may sincerely resist the evil one's methods of attack. Peace be to all and love with faith from God and our Lord Jesus Christ.

Second Sunday in Lent

Lections: Genesis 17:1-7, 15-16; Psalm 22:23-31; Romans 4:13-25; Mark 8:31-38 or Mark 9:2-9

Invocation

God of Abraham and Sarah,
Maker of an everlasting covenant,
may all the ends of the earth remember you today;
may those who seek to save their lives find abundant life in you;
may your kingdom come in power in every land.
We offer our praise and adoration
to the One who is faithful,
to the One who satisfies the poor,
to the One who raises us to new life.
As we wait in your presence, renew our faith,
restore our hope,
and revive our love.
We pray in the name of your Son, our Savior, Jesus Christ.
Amen.

Benediction

May the God who made Abraham and Sarah fruitful
and who raised Jesus to new life, fill you with hope,
strengthen your faith,
and make you righteous servants of the everlasting God.

Third Sunday in Lent

Lections: Exodus 20:1-17; Psalm 19; 1 Corinthians 1:18-25; John 2:13-22

Invocation

O Lord God, we acknowledge your presence here.
We gather in the name of Jesus,
Who established the church,
Who has shown us you, O God,
As no one has ever been able to, before or since,

Who has come into our lives
As a friend, redeemer, Savior and Lord,
And who utterly transforms
Each one who comes to you, O God,
Through Jesus Christ our Lord.
Do your transforming work today.
May your message be the power unto salvation,
As we gather in Jesus' name.

Benediction

"Now to him who by the power at work within us is able to accomplish abundantly far more than all we can ask or imagine, to him be glory in the church and in Christ Jesus to all generations, forever and ever" (Eph. 3:20-21).

Fourth Sunday in Lent

Lections: Numbers 21:4-9; Psalm 107:1-3, 17-22; Ephesians 2:1-10; John 3:14-21

Invocation

O God, you have gathered us in from many places, from the east and from the west, from the north and from the south. You have redeemed us as your people. When we have cried to you in the midst of our troubles, you have come to save us. You have delivered us from destruction. You have been rich in mercy.

We come to give thanks to you, O Lord; for you are good, for your steadfast love endures forever. Move among us by your Spirit this day, that we may worship you acceptably. Through Jesus Christ our Lord. Amen.

Benediction

By God's grace you have been saved. By God's grace you have been healed. By God's grace you have been made alive. By God's grace you have been raised with Christ Jesus—seated with him in heavenly places.

Go now with the assurance of God's grace upon your life—at home, at school, at work, at play. May Jesus meet your every need. Amen.

Fifth Sunday in Lent

Lections: Jeremiah 31:31-34; Psalm 51:1-12 or Psalm 119:9-16; Hebrews 5:5-10; John 12:20-33

Invocation

Come, O God, come.
For we who were one time far off,
Are drawn close by the sacrifice of Christ.
He is our peace
Who has made us one
And has broken down the wall between us.
And we come to you,
No more strangers or foreigners,
But fellow citizens with the saints
And as your household, your family,
Through Jesus Christ, our Savior and Lord.

Benediction

"May the God of peace make you holy through and through. May you be kept sound in spirit, mind and body, blameless until the coming of our Lord Jesus Christ. He who calls you is utterly faithful and he will finish what he has set out to do" (1 Thess. 5:23-24 JBP).

Passion/Palm Sunday

Lections: Isaiah 50:4-9*a*; Psalm 118:1-2, 19-29; Philippians 2:5-11; Mark 11:1-11

Invocation

Out of our need we come
Inviting your presence here today, O God.
We come out of our darkness to receive your light.
We come out of our sorrow to receive your joy.
We come out of our doubts to receive your certainty.
We come out of our anxiety to receive your peace.
We come out of failure and sin to receive your forgiveness.
Open our hearts so that you can open your hand
And satisfy our every need.
Through Jesus Christ we pray.

Benediction

Go forth in the forgiveness that is yours in Christ.
Go forth in the assurance of cleansing from all sin.
Go forth in claiming the victory of Christ
And the peace of Christ shall go with you.

Easter Season

Easter Day

Lections: Acts 10:34-43; Psalm 118:1-2, 14-24; 1 Corinthians 15:1-11; John 20:1-18

Invocation

Almighty God, you have sent Jesus into the world to suffer, die, and rise again. We rejoice today in so great a salvation and in the transforming power of Christ's resurrection in our lives, so that we can walk in the power of the Resurrection and in newness of life. Today, as your people, we pray for you to do your transforming work in each of our lives so that our lives, our work, our moments, and our days may be alive with the risen Christ.

Benediction

Go forth from here
And like Christ who was raised from the dead
By the glory of God
Even so, you shall walk in newness of life
Through the power of our living Lord.

Second Sunday of Easter

Lections: Acts 4:32-35; Psalm 133; 1 John 1:1–2:2; John 20:19-31

Invocation

O God, maker of all that is good, we rejoice in your goodness. Shine the light of your presence upon us this day that we may walk in fellowship with one another. May the peace of your presence unite us in fellowship as we worship and praise your high and holy name.

Benediction

Go with sins forgiven. Serve the Lord with gladness. Freely you have received; freely give.

Third Sunday of Easter

Lections: Acts 3:12-19; Psalm 4; 1 John 3:1-7; Luke 24:36*b*-48

Invocation

Grant, O God, that today and every time we come before you in united worship and prayer, we may be vividly aware of your presence among us. May we sense your power and protection and be revived to know deep within our hearts and minds and souls the wonder of your grace, peace, and love revealed through Jesus Christ our Lord.

Benediction

"Now the God of peace, who brought back from the dead that great shepherd of the sheep, our Lord Jesus, by the blood of the everlasting agreement, equip you thoroughly for the doing of [God's] will! May [the Creator] effect in us everything that pleases [God] through Jesus Christ, to whom be glory for ever and ever. Amen" (Heb. 13:20-21 JBP).

Fourth Sunday of Easter

Lections: Acts 4:5-12; Psalm 23; 1 John 3:16-24; John 10:11-18

Invocation

O Divine Shepherd, restore our souls.
You, who welcome us into your pastures of peacefulness and plenty, restore our souls.

You who travel through the dark valleys of Lent ahead of us and beside us, and also fill our spirits with the joy of Easter, restore our souls.

You, who know the workings of our minds and emotions better than we do ourselves, restore our souls.

Restore us through your Holy Spirit, the love of Jesus Christ, and the comfort of your presence. Amen.

Benediction

This is how you will know the love of Jesus Christ—by accepting it as a free and valued gift.

And this is how the world will know you are a child of Jesus Christ—by the way you love one another, in truth and in action.

Go in love. Amen.

Fifth Sunday of Easter

Lections: Acts 8:26-40; Psalm 22:25-31; 1 John 4:7-21; John 15:1-8

Invocation

We gather together today, O God, from our own small worlds, to worship unitedly in this place. We are here because of your love demonstrated supremely in Christ. Your grace binds us in fellowship. Your Spirit makes here a communion of faith. Keep us from thoughtless prayer, listless singing, or dull minds. Make this place today, a vantage point of spiritual insight from which we may go forth prepared to serve you and others.

Benediction

Depart as God's faithful stewards for the Scripture says, "There is no limit to the blessings which God can send you—[God] will make sure that you will always have all you need for yourselves in every possible circumstance, and still have something to spare for all sorts of good works" (2 Cor. 9:8 JB).

Sixth Sunday of Easter

Lections: Acts 10:44-48; Psalm 98; 1 John 5:1-6; John 15:9-17

Invocation

In this time of worship
We welcome you, O God.
We welcome you, O Christ.
We welcome you, O Holy Spirit.
Turn our minds unto you,
So that we may understand the true meaning of life.
Turn our hearts unto you
So that we may abide in your love
And your love may flow through us.
Turn our wills unto your Word
So that you may guide us into all truth.
Through Jesus Christ our Lord. Amen.

Benediction

"I pray . . . that God who gives you hope will keep you happy and full of peace as you believe in [God]. I pray that God will help you overflow with hope in [God] through the Holy Spirit's power within you" (Rom. 15:13 TLB).

Seventh Sunday of Easter

Lections: Acts 1:15-17, 21-26; Psalm 1; 1 John 5:9-13; John 17:6-19

Invocation

Lord Jesus, come,
  You, who have called us, each one
  Your Holy Spirit has spoken
    You have whispered our names
    You prosper our ways
    You enrich our days
    You give life eternal.
You prayed for us—
  Protection from the evil one
  Unity with Yourself and the Creator
  Sanctification by the truth.
Thank you. May our lives be as sturdy as trees planted by living water.

Benediction

Go forth from here as trees—strong and healthy!
Rooted and grounded in God's Word
Nurtured by God's grace
Watered and enabled by the power of the Holy Spirit
Blown and bent by enough distress to make you strong
God bless your going. Amen.

Season After Pentecost

Trinity Sunday
(First Sunday After Pentecost)

Lections: Isaiah 6:1-8; Psalm 29; Romans 8:12-17; John 3:1-17

Invocation

God, with what name shall we call you, as we enter this place of worship? And how might we ascribe to you all the glory due your name? You are "awesome," we say. Yet all our attempts at knowing you are faint reflections of your holy splendor.

We all too often come with apathy into this place of worship; we hardly expect to meet our God.

Shake us up, Lord! We want to see a bit of that smoke and fire that Isaiah saw. Shake us up out of the lethargy of indifference, until we see you fill this place with your very presence, Lord. Amen.

Benediction

Here we have been in the presence of God. We have heard a word from the Lord. And the Lord is saying: "Whom shall I send?"

So go from this place, having been changed. Go from this place, ready to serve. Go with the words on your lips, "Here am I, send me."

Sunday Between May 29 and June 4 Inclusive (if after Trinity Sunday)

Lections: 1 Samuel 3:1-10, (11-20); Psalm 139:1-6, 13-18; 2 Corinthians 4:5-12; Mark 2:23–3:6

Invocation

Lord, it's Sunday again. And it seems right to be here and to worship you. You've commanded that we have no other "gods" this week—"gods" of work, success, and pleasure. We set aside this time to worship you alone.

We've turned to you in glimmerings and flickerings throughout the week. Now we want to devote our concentration to you. Be pleased with our worship. Hear our prayers. Speak to us through your Word and your Holy Spirit. Redeem the clutterings of our lives. Inspire us from the mundaneness of our religious meanderings to a brisk spiritual walk.

May this be a holy hour. A set apart time. A service of worship to you our Lord and God. In the name of the Father and the Son and the Holy Spirit. Amen.

Benediction

We rejoice in this Lord's day service. It has been good to rest, worship, and to meditate on you, gracious God. While we can't set aside all week to worship you in this way, help us to take an ever-present spirit of worship, fellowship, and Christian devotion with us throughout our week. Guide our steps. Pervade our thoughts. Keep us close to you by your Spirit. May we be strengthened by your love and in turn may our lives be an extension of your love to others.

And may the mercy, grace, and peace of our Lord Jesus Christ be with each of us as we go on our way. Amen.

Sunday Between June 5 and June 11 Inclusive (if after Trinity Sunday)

Lections: 1 Samuel 8:4-11, (12-15), 16-20, (11:14-15); Psalm 138; 2 Corinthians 4:13–5:1; Mark 3:20-35

Invocation

O God, whose ways are just—
We are your people. We place ourselves under your rule.
Our souls wait for you, and in your Word we hope.

Your truth is eternal; your grace extends to all people.
In this hour we come to you alone for truth.
We come to you alone for grace.
We live only by your truth and your grace.
Through Jesus Christ our Lord.

Benediction

We have been in the presence of the God of truth and grace.
We have seen glimpses of God's vision for our world.
Now we go forth to the grit and grime of our daily lives.

As we live in the tension between God's vision for our world,
May God provide discernment that we may truly know the ways of the Lord,
and power to work for justice and eternal truth.
May God's Spirit renew our inner nature day by day, so that we do not lose heart.

Sunday Between June 12 and June 18 Inclusive (if after Trinity Sunday)

Lections: 1 Samuel 15:34–16:13; Psalm 20; 2 Corinthians 5:6-10, (11-13), 14-17; Mark 4:26-34

Invocation

It is good to be here, today, Lord!
It is good to praise your Holy Name!

Our songs of joy celebrate your Love
in the morning.
Our words of praise proclaim your faithfulness
at night.
You have granted us VICTORY!
O Lord, praise your Holy Name! Amen.

Benediction

May the seed planted today
sprout and grow.
May the resulting plant
bear fruit.
First the stalk, then the head, and finally the full kernel!

Go forth as sowers of the precious seed—
Sowers in the kingdom.
And grant, God, that your kingdom may begin in us. Amen.

Sunday Between June 19 and
June 25 Inclusive (if after Trinity Sunday)

Lections: 1 Samuel 17:(1*a*, 4-11, 19-23), 32-49; Psalm 9:9-20;
2 Corinthians 6:1-13; Mark 4:35-41

Invocation

Come to us, O Christ
Forgive our feeble faith,
When the winds of life become blustery
And the waves seem to overtake us.
In this hour of worship
Send forth fresh courage
And then send us forth
In full confidence in your Word, O Christ.

Benediction

May the grace of Christ
That daily renews our lives,
And the love of God
That enables us to love all persons,
And the fellowship of the Holy Spirit
That unites us as one body,
Make us keen to discern
And prompt to obey
The complete will of God
Until we meet again, through Jesus Christ our Lord.

Sunday Between June 26 and July 2 Inclusive

Lections: 2 Samuel 1:1, 17-27; Psalm 130; 2 Corinthians 8:7-15;
Mark 5:21-43

Invocation

O God, as we gather today, take the small seed planted and
make it bear abundant fruit. Take some word or phrase, be
it spoken or sung, and use it to enlighten and strengthen so
that we may leave here today with renewed faith and restored strength and confidence in our living Lord.

Benediction

And now may the power of our God
And of the Lord Jesus Christ
And the power of the Holy Spirit
Go with you always and in all ways.

Sunday Between July 3 and July 9 Inclusive

Lections: 2 Samuel 5:1-5, 9-10; Psalm 48; 2 Corinthians 12:2-10; Mark 6:1-13

Invocation

LEADER: You enter a familiar place with your friends—let it not be too familiar. Jesus could not perform miracles in a familiar place, his hometown and his synagogue. About these he said:

PEOPLE: **"Only in his home town and in his own house is a prophet without honor."**

LEADER: Jesus instead left his familiar place and went to the unfamiliar. There in villages and towns he drove out demons, anointed many sick people with oil and healed them.

PEOPLE: **Guard us from becoming too familiar because of past involvements with this place and this people. We do not ask for adversity but humility, for you have said: "My grace is sufficient for you, for my power is made perfect in weakness."**

LEADER: O God, enter now this house and give to us power to heal and forgive as we worship you.

Benediction

People of God, the Lord sends you into the world, to a harsh and oftentimes cruel place. Many do not live by the same values as you; many do not know you. The world in which you enter is oftentimes obstinate and stubborn. You, however, are different. By word and deed share what the Lord has done. And whether the world listens or not they will know that a Christian has been among them.

Sunday Between July 10 and July 16 Inclusive

Lections: 2 Samuel 6:1-5, 12*b*-19; Psalm 24; Ephesians 1:3-14; Mark 6:14-29

Invocation

The earth is the Lord's and all that is in it; the world, and those who live in it.
Our sovereign Lord,
who has founded the seas and established the rivers,
placed the hills and formed the valleys,
We lift up our heads this day in praise and thanksgiving.
Blessed are you, God, maker of heaven and earth,
who long before you ever laid down earth's foundation,
had us on mind, and decided to adopt us into your family
through the sacrifice of your Son, Jesus.
Blessed are you O God, maker of heaven and earth, and
Blessed are those who have come seeking.
The earth is the Lord's and all that is in it; the world, and those who live in it. Amen.

Benediction

Blessed be the God of our Lord Jesus Christ,
Who blesses us, chooses us, adopts us as children,
Who forgives our sins, redeems us, and lavishes full grace on us.
Go now with clean hands and pure hearts,
Proclaiming the love and mystery of God's will.

Sunday Between July 17 and July 23 Inclusive

Lections: 2 Samuel 7:1-14*a*; Psalm 89:20-37; Ephesians 2:11-22; Mark 6:30-34, 53-56

Invocation

Merciful and loving God,
Even as our Lord needed times alone,
So we need this time
Away from work and busyness.
We want to be vividly aware
Of your presence.
We want to become more conscious of your power.
We need to sense
Your protection.
We desire to know more fully
The wonder of your presence.

Benediction

"May the LORD give strength to his people!
May the LORD bless his people with peace!" (Ps. 29:11)

Sunday Between July 24 and July 30 Inclusive

Lections: 2 Samuel 11:1-15; Psalm 14; Ephesians 3:14-21; John 6:1-21

Invocation

O God, lead us in our worship today
That our lips might praise you,
Our lives might bless you,

And our thoughts might glorify your name.
We come to sing and to pray,
Knowing that you always hear us.
Help us to hear you.
In the name of Jesus. Amen.

Benediction

God is at work in the world. Even in the most barren places, God watches over us and walks with us. And so as Jesus faced temptation with the Word of God, let us also face the challenges of our own lives with God's Word. Go out with the conviction that we do not live by bread alone, but by every word from the mouth of God. Worship and serve the Lord, and go in peace. Amen.

Sunday Between July 31 and August 6 Inclusive

Lections: 2 Samuel 11:26–12:13*a*; Psalm 51:1-12; Ephesians 4:1-16; John 6:24-35

Invocation

Lord, we gather as your people, the body of Christ in the world. We are here because of the faithfulness of others down through the years. We thank you that no time has ever lacked voices to tell your story. And you continue to empower those who serve you today. Make us faithful witnesses. Allow no spectators. Help us to hear and to do your good will today as we gather and as we go.

Benediction

And now "The grace of the Lord Jesus Christ, the love of God, and the fellowship that is ours in the Holy Spirit be with you all!" (2 Cor. 13:14 JBP).

Sunday Between August 7 and August 13 Inclusive

Lections: 2 Samuel 18:5-9, 15, 31-33; Psalm 130; Ephesians 4:25–5:2; John 6:35, 41-51

Invocation

We welcome you, O God, to this hour of worship. We need the light of your presence. Reveal yourself to us so that we may better see you and love you. Strengthen our wills so that we choose the good over the evil. Show us the glory and the power of the blessed gospel, made known to us through your Son, Jesus Christ. Teach us to live in love as Christ has loved us.

Benediction

"May the God of peace make you perfect and holy; and may you all be kept safe and blameless, spirit, soul and body, for the coming of our Lord Jesus Christ. God has called you and [God] will not fail you" (1 Thess. 5:23-24 JB).

Sunday Between August 14 and August 20 Inclusive

Lections: 1 Kings 2:10-12; 3:3-14; Psalm 111; Ephesians 5:15-20; John 6:51-58

Invocation

From the rising of the sun to its setting, O Lord, your name is to be praised. We are here gathered to join in that praise. Make this a holy hour. Make it also a happy, joyful time of praise and sincere worship. Stir us by your Spirit so that none may stay without an awareness of your presence and love and none may leave without a sense of your accompaniment in the details and decisions of each day ahead.

Benediction

You have met for worship.
Go forth to witness.
You have met to hear the Word of God.
Go forth to share that Word.
You have met as God's people.
Go forth as Christ's body.

Sunday Between August 21 and August 27 Inclusive

Lections: 1 Kings 8:(1, 6, 10-11), 22-30, 41-43; Psalm 84; Ephesians 6:10-20; John 6:56-69

Invocation

O Lord, our Lord, you are the Creator and Sustainer of us all. Today we want to worship you with gladness and come into your presence with singing. We invoke your presence among us today so that none who leave this place will leave without the deep assurance of your love, without the strong confidence of your faithfulness, without a fresh and full commitment to live by your power and for your glory.

Benediction

"Finally, be strong in the Lord and in the strength of [God's] power. Put on the whole armor of God, so that you may be able to stand against the wiles of the devil" (Eph. 6:10-11).

Sunday Between August 28 and September 3 Inclusive

Lections: Song of Solomon 2:8-13; Psalm 45:1-2, 6-9; James 1:17-27; Mark 7:1-8, 14-15, 21-23

Invocation

Eternal Creator, you have been good, beyond all deserving. All we have and are is the gift of your love. You have surrounded us with your light and your love, with beauty and with friends. You have placed hope in our hearts. As we unite in worship, make us alert to every desire you have for us. Where our hearts are hardened, soften them. Where our minds are closed to your truth, open them. Where our feet are slow to follow you, spur us on. Do all of this and more, as you know our need, in this time of worship together.

Benediction

Go forth as doers of the Word,
Not forgetting what you have heard,
and as the Scripture has promised
"You will be blessed in your doing."

Sunday Between September 4 and September 10 Inclusive

Lections: Proverbs 22:1-2, 8-9, 22-23; Psalm 125; James 2:1-10, (11-13), 14-17; Mark 7:24-37

Invocation

Come Lord God among us.
Give light to our minds, which hunger for truth.
Give peace to our hearts, which hunger for rest.

Give strength to our spirits, which hunger for help.
Renew your work of grace and salvation
Within us as we join in worship,
So that we may go from here
Strong in your strength to be your people
To do your will. Through our Lord Jesus Christ.

Benediction

"May the God of hope fill you with all joy and peace in your faith, that by the power of the Holy Spirit, your whole life and outlook may be radiant with hope" (Rom. 15:13 JBP).

Sunday Between September 11 and September 17 Inclusive

Lections: Proverbs 1:20-33; Psalm 19 or Wisdom of Solomon 7:26–8:1; James 3:1-12; Mark 8:27-38

Invocation

Eternal and loving Creator, today we join with the millions around your world in worship. Wherever your people meet, make your presence known and open the hearts of your people. And give to us who gather here in these moments a united response of mind and heart to you and your will. We ask, O God, that our lips and our lives may join in confessing clearly the gospel we profess.
Take the dimness from our eyes
And enlighten our minds by your Word.
Quicken our hearts by your Spirit
And lead our steps in the way everlasting.

Benediction

"Now may the Lord of peace himself give you peace at all times in all ways. The Lord be with all of you" (2 Thess. 3:16).

Sunday Between September 18 and September 24 Inclusive

Lections: Proverbs 31:10-31; Psalm 1; James 3:13–4:3, 7-8*a*; Mark 9:30-37

Invocation

Who is the greatest among us? Who is the wisest? Who is the most righteous? Who is the most precious? These are earthly questions, human questions. But in your eyes, O God, all are precious. Through the work of Jesus, all may be made righteous. In the humility of the Spirit, all may find wisdom and true greatness. O great and wise God, the all righteous and most precious, receive our worship. Lead us to a deeper understanding of you as our Creator and of ourselves as your creation. For we ask in the righteous name of Jesus. Amen.

Benediction

Together we have worshiped. Together we stand ready to serve. May we be rooted in the Word of God. May we blossom with faith and good works. May we delight in the Lord, and may our Lord take delight in us. Amen.

Sunday Between September 25 and October 1 Inclusive

Lections: Esther 7:1-6, 9-10; 9:20-22; Psalm 124; James 5:13-20; Mark 9:38-50

Invocation

LEADER: Praise the Lord!

PEOPLE: Praise the Lord, O my soul!

LEADER: I will praise the Lord as long as I live.

PEOPLE:	**Praise the Lord, O my soul!**
LEADER:	Praise the Lord who made the heaven and earth, the sea and all that live there.
PEOPLE:	**Praise the Lord, O my soul!**
LEADER:	Praise the Lord who executes justice and keeps faith forever.
PEOPLE:	**Praise the Lord, O my soul!**
LEADER:	Praise the Lord who will reign forever and ever.
PEOPLE:	**Praise the Lord, O my soul!**

Benediction

Wherever you go from here, whatever you experience,
God is with you.
Store up for yourselves the rich treasures of Jesus Christ; be
rich in good works, generous, and ready to share,
So that you may take hold of the life that really is life.
Amen.

Sunday Between October 2 and October 8 Inclusive

Lections: Job 1:1; 2:1-10; Psalm 26; Hebrews 1:1-4; 2:5-12;
Mark 10:2-16

Invocation

God of glory,
And Savior of us all,
We join today the cloud of witnesses
Of the past and present.
You have spoken to us your message in Jesus.

You have gathered us as your visible body in Christ.
Confirm your calling for each of us
And make our fellowship rich
With all your saints on earth and in heaven.

Benediction

"Now to him who is able to do immeasurably more than all
we can ask or conceive, by the power which is at work
among us, to him be glory in the church and in Christ Jesus
from generation to generation evermore! Amen" (Eph. 3:20-
21 NEB).

Sunday Between October 9 and October 15 Inclusive

Lections: Job 23:1-9, 16-17; Psalm 22:1-15; Hebrews 4:12-16;
Mark 10:17-31

Invocation

Speak your Word to each of us, O God
Before your Word none remain hidden.
Reach out to the lost.
Restore the fallen.
Rebuke the proud.
Remember the discouraged.
Revive our spirits.
Remold our lives to the likeness of Christ.
In whose name we pray.

Benediction

You have come close to us in Christ,
You have shown us your love, grace, and compassion.
As we go from here
Give us your patience when people are indifferent.

Give us your compassion when people are in need.
Give us your love to reflect your grace and forgiveness.

Sunday Between October 16 and October 22 Inclusive

Lections: Job 38:1-7, (34-41); Psalm 104:1-9, 24, 35*c*; Hebrews 5:1-10; Mark 10:35-45

Invocation

Eternal God,
Worshiped and served by the hosts of heaven,
Come near to us,
Who seek to worship and serve you on earth.
Without your aid
We get our values and priorities mixed up.
We cannot worship or work in ways pleasing to you.
But with your presence and blessing
All life will be radiant.
Come near to us we pray
For we ask all in and through the merits of your Son, Jesus Christ.

Benediction

Go from here strengthened in your inner being,
Be established in love,
So that everyone you meet
May be touched by Christ's love,
As you serve one another
In the humility and grace of Jesus Christ.

Sunday Between October 23 and October 29 Inclusive

Lections: Job 42:1-6, 10-17; Psalm 34:1-8, (19-22); Hebrews 7:23-28; Mark 10:46-52

Invocation

Today, again, O God
We come in assurance and hope.
We come because of your promise
To save, for all time,
All those who come to you
Through Jesus Christ.
We thank you for Christ's intercession
On our behalf.
We are here
Because we believe in the communion of saints,
Because we believe in the forgiveness of sins
Because we believe in the resurrection of life here and here-after.
Strengthen this assurance and hope today.
For it is through Christ we pray.

Benediction

"The Lord is faithful, and he will give you strength and guard you from the evil one, and we, in the Lord, have every confidence that you are doing and will go on doing all that we tell you. May the Lord turn your hearts toward the love of God and the fortitude of Christ" (2 Thess. 3:3-5 JB).

Sunday Between October 30 and November 5 Inclusive

Lections: Ruth 1:1-18; Psalm 146; Hebrews 9:11-14; Mark 12:28-34

Invocation

Listen up, everyone! Our God is One God,
Whose love for us is One Love,
Larger than the Universe, Longer than Eternity.
The "buck" stops at God's throne!
Let us bring our God an offering of
all our love, with all our heart,
all our devotion, with all our soul,
all our activity, with all our strength.
Let us bow down in one accord.
Let us come as one to the feet of the One God, our Lord.
Amen.

Benediction

Go from this place
with God's righteous yearnings for you etched upon your mind.
Tie them as memos on your finger—lest you forget.
Go from this place remembering that
Our God remains faithful forever.
Our God provides.
Our God watches over us.
Our God reigns forever. Amen.

Sunday Between November 6 and November 12 Inclusive

Lections: Ruth 3:1-5; 4:13-17; Psalm 127; Hebrews 9:24-28; Mark 12:38-44

Invocation

Today we gather as Christ's body, the beloved community of memory and hope, of love and of faith. You are our help in the past and our hope for years to come, O God. We thank you that we are here as a perpetual witness to your salvation and a witness to our own generation of your truth, love, and the hope of your coming again.

Benediction

"May the God of peace . . . sanctify you entirely; and may your spirit and soul and body be kept sound and blameless at the coming of our Lord Jesus Christ. The one who calls you is faithful, and he will do this" (1 Thess. 5:23-24).

Sunday Between November 13 and November 19 Inclusive

Lections: 1 Samuel 1:4-20; 1 Samuel 2:1-10; Hebrews 10:11-14, (15-18), 19-25; Mark 13:1-8

Invocation

Our Heavenly Creator, we praise you for this, another privilege of worship. And we thank you for this church that you have entrusted with the rich treasure of the gospel of Christ. We are grateful today for those who have passed on the faith in the past and who are a cloud of witnesses to our gathering here. May we also be led in the true and living way and keep the covenants that we have made to you. Place your love in our hearts we pray, and write your Word on our minds. Give us the assurance of your forgiveness and fill our hearts with praise.

Benediction

"To him who loves us and freed us from our sins by his blood, and made us to be a kingdom, priests serving his God and Father, to him be glory and dominion forever and ever. Amen" (Rev. 1:5b-6).

Reign of Christ/Christ the King Sunday

Lections: 2 Samuel 23:1-7; Psalm 132:1-12, (13-18); Revelation 1:4b-8; John 18:33-37

Invocation

Almighty God, you have established your throne in the heavens.
May your kingdom come,
And your will be done,
On earth as it is in heaven.
Rule in our hearts through Jesus Christ,
That we may rejoice in our salvation through his lordship.
Amen.

Benediction

You are a royal priesthood,
A holy nation, a people belonging to God.
Go now to serve in God's kingdom through the strength,
The love, and the enduring presence
Of Jesus Christ our Lord. Amen.

Year C

Advent Season

....

First Sunday of Advent

Lections: Jeremiah 33:14-16; Psalm 25:1-10; 1 Thessalonians
3:9-13; Luke 21:25-36

Invocation

Gracious Holy Spirit, we sit here pondering
The beginning of the Christmas season.
To you, Lord, we lift up our souls. Clear out the dread
of days to come;
Wash away the shame of days poorly spent;
Teach us the joy of days prayerfully ordered.
Make our love for one another increase and
overflow.
To you, Lord, we lift up our souls.

Benediction

Good and upright Lord!
How we love you for being everything we
could be!
O Lord, let us become leaves on that righteous
branch
Of the vine, leaves on a fruitful fig tree.
Thank you for tomorrow, for all its possibilities,
For all its signs and wonders, pointing to your presence in
our world.
O Lord, we are standing because you have taught us to walk
in your way,
And to watch and pray for your coming without fear or
apprehension.
You are very near and we long to see you
face-to-face.

Second Sunday of Advent

Lections: Baruch 5:1-9 or Malachi 3:1-4; Luke 1:68-79; Philippians 1:3-11; Luke 3:1-6

Invocation

Gracious God, we gather today in this Advent season. We desire to live our lives in your presence, but sometimes our busyness keeps us from hearing your voice.

We are getting ready for Christmas, but sometimes we neglect to get ready to receive the Christ of Christmas into our very lives.

Now we lay aside the frenzied whirlwind of activity, to once again hear your small voice.

We have come here by many paths, and the road this week has not always been smooth. In the midst of all the vagaries of life, we trust that we, with all humankind, will see God's salvation.

"Cast out our sin and enter in, be born in us today," we pray in Jesus' name. Amen.

Benediction

Here in this place we have seen an intimation of the presence of Christ. As we leave this place of worship, we once again meet ourselves. Help us to see Christ in each of our brothers and sisters. And as we encounter a needy world, may we do our part to make the rough places smooth, so those around us will see God's saving work.

Third Sunday of Advent

Lections: Zephaniah 3:14-20; Isaiah 12:2-6; Philippians 4:4-7; Luke 3:7-18

Invocation

O God, vitalize the worship of your people today by your presence. Impart to us the thrill of singing from the heart the great songs of the ages. Move us to the depth of true gratitude and expectation by the words of our Lord, "Where two or three are gathered together in my name, there am I in the midst of them" (Matt. 18:20 KJV). May we know the wonder of true worship today, together. May your peace that passes all understanding, guard our hearts and minds, through Christ Jesus.

Benediction

Beloved of the Lord, go from here
With rejoicing.
Let your gentleness be known to all.
The Lord is always by your side.
Cast worry aside.
And by prayer and petition,
With thanksgiving,
Let your requests be made known to God.
And the peace of God will keep you.

Fourth Sunday of Advent

Lections: Micah 5:2-5*a*; Luke 1:47-55 or Psalm 80:1-7; Hebrews 10:5-10; Luke 1:39-45, (46-55)

Invocation

Come, thou long expected Jesus.
We, along with those of every age,
And, along with all those who join in worship this day,
Around the world, expect you, O Christ,
To be present with us,
For you have come in your birth in Bethlehem.

And you are present
Wherever your church comes together.
Renew our awareness of your coming, then and now.

Benediction

Go from this place of worship,
Knowing that you also
Are blessed of the Lord.
Christ whose presence is among us,
Go with each of you,
Into your home and community,
Into your work and play,
Until you can say, wherever you move,
"Surely the Lord is in this place."

Christmas Season

First Sunday After Christmas Day

Lections: 1 Samuel 2:18-20, 26; Psalm 148; Colossians 3:12-17;
Luke 2:41-52

Invocation

As in the days of our youth, O Lord, we come expectantly,
anticipating what you have in store for us this day. We're
eager to hear your voice, and ready to hear your call. As the
excitement of the season lingers, yet giving way to the anticipation of a new year, we come to worship and adore you still.
Clothe us in righteousness and compassion. May the unity
of the Spirit pervade our worship together. Lift our hearts.
Renew our spirits. Let us dwell upon your Word.
  We ask your blessing upon our service. In the name of the
Lord Jesus. Amen.

Benediction

There's a void to the stillness at the end of this season. As our
fellowship is concluded and we leave this sanctuary, we go
from here to the strange dullness of the after-Christmas lull
combined with the hesitant anxiousness of beginning a new
year.
Yet even in the midst of this sentimental turmoil, the peace
of Christ can settle, calm, and enliven our depressing anxiousness.
May our lives be enriched by all that is good. May our
fellowship be sweetened by sincerity and kindness. And may
the reality of the blessedness of the Christian life bring an
ever present glow to our hearts.
Through Jesus Christ our Lord. Amen.

Second Sunday After Christmas Day

Lections: Jeremiah 31:7-14; Psalm 147:12-20; Ephesians 1:3-14; John 1:(1-9), 10-18

Invocation

Come to us, O God,
In our time together.
You are the source of every spiritual blessing.
You have chosen us in Christ.
You have adopted us into your family.
You have redeemed and forgiven us,
According to the riches of your grace.
And, as we are here by your mercy and grace,
Make us conscious anew of your blessings.
But, above all, O God,
Make us conscious of you, the Blesser,
The giver of every good and perfect gift,
And the giver of your only Son, Jesus,
Through whom we pray it all. Amen.

Benediction

Now may God who has begun a good work in you, continue to work in you his perfect will, even as he promised, so that you may fulfill God's purpose with joy and have a sense of his presence with you always.

Season After the Epiphany

....

Baptism of the Lord
(First Sunday After the Epiphany)

Lections: Isaiah 43:1-7; Psalm 29; Acts 8:14-17; Luke 3:15-17, 21-22

Invocation

Lord, our Lord, enthroned above the storms of our lives,
As we gather in the shadow of your awesome splendor,
Shake our deserts of despair.
Strip bare the forest of our transgressions.
And out of your strength, Lord, bless your people with peace.
O Holy Spirit, come on the quiet wings of a dove
With gentle tenderness,
And caress our lifted faces with the wingbeats of your love.
O Holy Spirit, come as unquenchable fire
With purifying heat
And cleanse the chaff from our hearts.
O Holy Spirit, come as thunder upon our apathy
With awesome swiftness
And strike us with the flash of lightning
Send us forth in POWER! Amen.

Benediction

Lord, our hearts are bent to receive your baptism!
Wash our thirsty, dusty hearts with rainsheets from heaven.
Send us forth thirst-quenched, refreshed, in the rainbow light
of Holy Spirit Power. Amen.

Second Sunday After the Epiphany

Lections: Isaiah 62:1-5; Psalm 36:5-10; 1 Corinthians 12:1-11; John 2:1-11

Invocation

Gracious God, we come to you in confidence. As you called and walked with your people in ages past, so too have you called us and walked with us. We praise you for your great goodness. We await what you would say to us during this time of worship. Open our hearts, loosen our lips, clear our minds, and dispel our anxieties that we may praise you and experience the miracle of your divine grace. Through Jesus, our Lord and Savior, we pray. Amen.

Benediction

May the God of Abraham and Sarah,
Isaac and Rebekah,
Moses, Miriam, and Aaron,
give you confidence to live according to God's holy way. May Jesus, the Christ, give you joy and peace for all your daily tasks. May the Holy Spirit guide and protect you from sin and danger. Amen.

Third Sunday After the Epiphany

Lections: Nehemiah 8:1-3, 5-6, 8-10; Psalm 19; 1 Corinthians 12:12-31*a*; Luke 4:14-21

Invocation

Lord God, we have come to worship and to hear what you want to say to us. Permit no spectators in this church. Move us, by your Spirit, as hearers to become doers. May each of us fulfill the ministry to which you have called, for each has received a gift. Each is a part of your body. Call us to recognize each gift and to minister to the varied gifts of each person, even as we stand in awe of such trust and responsibility.

Benediction

Go from here, in the Spirit and power of Christ,
To share the good news,
To proclaim release to the captives,
Recovery of sight to the blind,
To let the oppressed go free,
To proclaim the year of the Lord's favor.
And as you go
Fulfilling Christ's mission
The living Christ will be with you.

Fourth Sunday After the Epiphany

Lections: Jeremiah 1:4-10; Psalm 71:1-6; 1 Corinthians 13:1-13; Luke 4:21-30

Invocation

Our God and Creator, we rejoice that you have created each one
With the capacity to love you
And to love one another.
Awaken such love for you
That we may know you better
Than our own flesh.
Quicken our love for others
So that our capacity to care,
To understand and to share,
May increase greatly.
May no ill feeling or action toward another

Prostitute the capacity
You have given each person here to love.

Benediction

"May the Lord direct your hearts to the love of God and to the steadfastness of Christ" (2 Thess. 3:5).

Fifth Sunday After the Epiphany

Lections: Isaiah 6:1-8, (9-13); Psalm 138; 1 Corinthians 15:1-11; Luke 5:1-11

Invocation

O Lord God,
You withhold no good thing from those who seek to serve you. Today we want to hear your call to each of us.
May we today know the richness of spiritual renewal.
May we today know the praise of joyful hearts.
May we today know the love of obedient lives.
May we today know the peace of Christ's presence.
Above all, open our minds and spirits to receive the good you so much want to give us today and to answer your call in Christ.

Benediction

Go forth from here
As those who hear the call of Christ,
As those who respond to that call,
As those who live in the high calling of God
In Christ Jesus.
And may the knowledge and forgiveness of Christ
Be shed abroad
Wherever you move.

Sixth Sunday After the Epiphany

Lections: Jeremiah 17:5-10; Psalm 1; 1 Corinthians 15:12-20; Luke 6:17-26

Invocation

Lord God,
We know something of the blessedness
Of knowing you,
And praising you.
Come among us now
As your people.
You are the opener of minds and hearts.
Open our minds to your truth.
Open our hearts in obedience and love.
Teach us anew
Your way of blessedness and life.

Benediction

And now may the rich blessings of God
And the grace of our Lord Jesus Christ
And the abiding presence of the Holy Spirit
Go with you
And be yours in increasing measure.

Seventh Sunday After the Epiphany

Lections: Genesis 45:3-11, 15; Psalm 37:1-11, 39-40; 1 Corinthians 15:35-38, 42-50; Luke 6:27-38

Invocation

Lord, we come together before you, with busy minds. Help us to accept your invitation to "be still."
We come with plans for later today and the coming week.

Help us to learn more of what it means when you say, "Trust in me."

We come with questions about life. Help us to wait patiently before you. We pray this in Jesus' name. Amen.

Benediction

Go forth into the world, sure of your salvation in Christ,
for the Lord has given it to you;
Secure in who holds you,
for God has rescued you;
Patient in your duties,
for God will use you.
Amen.

Eighth Sunday After the Epiphany

Lections: Sirach 27:4-7; Psalm 92:1-4, 12-15; 1 Corinthians 15:51-58; Luke 6:39-49

Invocation

LEFT: **We gather today to lead one another to you, O God. Come among us.**

RIGHT: **We gather today to learn what it means to follow you, O God.**

LEADER: A student is not above the teacher, but everyone who is full trained will be like the teacher.

LEFT: **We gather today to listen to what you, O God, are revealing through the circumstance of life.**

RIGHT: **We gather today to repent from our judgmental habits.**

LEADER: Do not look at the speck of sawdust in your brother's or sister's eye. Pay attention to the plank in your own eye, then you remove the speck from your neighbor's eye.

LEFT: We gather to discover the meaning of living with the fruit of the Spirit.

RIGHT: We gather to help one another walk in the Spirit.

LEADER: Each tree is recognized by its own fruit just as the good person brings good things out of the good stored up in the heart. Out of the overflow of the heart the mouth speaks.

Benediction

My dear brothers and sisters, as you leave this place, stand firm. Let nothing move you. Always give yourself fully to the work of the Lord, because you know that your labor in the Lord is not in vain. Go in peace.

Ninth Sunday After the Epiphany

Lections: 1 Kings 8:22-23, 41-43; Psalm 96:1-9; Galatians 1:1-12; Luke 7:1-10

Invocation

O God, Lord of heaven and earth,
You have revealed yourself to us in Jesus Christ.
You have come to us in your Holy Spirit.
You have come to us through your body, the church.
Today as we gather, as your people,
Increase our understanding of who you are,
And of your will for each of us,
So that our feeble faith may grow in the grace and knowledge

Of our Lord Jesus Christ.
We invoke your presence and power
So that we may live by love,
And walk by faith.

Benediction

"Peace be to the whole community, and love with faith, from God the [Creator] and the Lord Jesus Christ. Grace be with all who have an undying love for our Lord Jesus Christ" (Eph. 6:23-24).

Last Sunday After the Epiphany
(Transfiguration Sunday)

Lections: Exodus 34:29-35; Psalm 99; 2 Corinthians 3:12–4:2; Luke 9:28-36, (37-43)

Invocation

Dear God,
How are you? We are fine!
Because you answered when people like Moses, Aaron, and Samuel asked, we know you will speak to us.
We can trust you.
We can be bold to ask.
Because you sent your Spirit to give hope,
We can be very bold.
We can be free to reflect your glory and to set forth the truth boldly.
Our clarity of witness can be a conscience to others.
You're great, Lord, and we are fine.
Thanks!

Benediction

Holy Spirit of God, you have reached into the lives of many biblical characters and transformed them. Your work continues today.

Some days are awed and humbled in the presence of your work. Some days you make a difference in whispers and small ways.

Help us always to be in awe of your power—and your gentleness.

Lead us to truth, and to freedom. Amen.

Lenten Season

....

First Sunday in Lent

Lections: Deuteronomy 26:1-11; Psalm 91:1-2, 9-16; Romans 10:8*b*-13; Luke 4:1-13

Invocation

Let us come together in the house of God, to worship the Lord, our God.
Let us come—recognizing ourselves as pilgrims protected by the strong arm of God, confessing with our mouths our utter dependence on God, pondering
within our hearts both our faith and our doubt, and always calling on the name of our Lord Jesus,
Let us come to celebrate all the bounty that the Lord our God is continually giving to us. Let us bring our gifts of thanksgiving before the Lord.
Together with all who call on the name of the Lord, from every race and nation we come to receive the Lord's protection from the evils of our world, to sense the loving presence of our Lord in times of trouble, and to seek the grace of salvation this day flowing freely from the One we confess as Lord.

Benediction

We have professed our faith here in the presence of brothers and sisters.
We have offered both ourselves and our possessions as gifts to our God.
And we have received from the Lord's hand bountiful mercy and grace.

Let us go forth to continue this cycle of giving and receiving, as we celebrate and live each day the faith we have professed this morning.
May our hearts and voices be continually before our Lord.
May we dwell in the shelter of the Almighty, and walk in God's presence with joy.

Second Sunday in Lent

Lections: Genesis 15:1-12, 17-18; Psalm 27; Philippians 3:17–4:1; Luke 13:31-35

Invocation

Enter among us this day, O God.
Where we are barren of faith,
Perform your miracle of truth.
Where we are barren of love,
Perform your miracle of grace.
Where we are barren of energy,
Perform your miracle of renewal.
Through Jesus Christ, our Lord

Benediction

Go with us, O God, in the shelter house of your protection.
Let us dwell in your presence this coming week,
So that we can be instruments for gathering your people
Through the respect and love we show to all we meet.
Amen.

Third Sunday in Lent

Lections: Isaiah 55:1-9; Psalm 63:1-8; 1 Corinthians 10:1-13; Luke 13:1-9

Invocation

Come near to us, O God.
We seek you and call upon you.
We need your mercy and pardon.
We come thirsty and wait upon you
Who gives the living water of life.
You are our rock and deliverer.
Turn us from every sin.
Teach us true repentance,
So that we may be
Neither barren or unfruitful,
But believe in our hearts,
And confess with our lips
Your salvation in Jesus Christ.

Benediction

Go from this place
Knowing that the Christ you met here goes with you.
Receive from him the living water, which refreshes you
And all whom you meet.

Fourth Sunday in Lent

Lections: Joshua 5:9-12; Psalm 32; 2 Corinthians 5:16-21; Luke 15:1-3, 11*b*-32

Invocation

Great God of steadfast love, come among us. We come to you this day with grateful hearts. You have reconciled us through your Son Jesus. Everything old has passed away; behold all has become new! Thank you God, for your provision and care for us. And yet we come also longing for peace; for reconciliation in our world, in our families, in our churches, and in our own hearts. Our strength is nearly dried up, our hearts are heavy, and the way seems hard. Come to us. Gather us in, and hold us in your arms of everlasting peace. You are a hiding place for us, and you keep us from trouble. Make the way clear, and teach us in the ways of reconciliation. Empower us to be your ambassadors for peace— agents of your love in this world. In the name of Jesus Christ, the Reconciler. Amen.

Benediction

Hide no more.
You have been reconciled.
Old things have passed away, behold everything has become new.
Rejoice. Be glad.
Now, God has given us the ministry of reconciliation.
We are the ambassadors of God's peace.
Be thankful and take courage. Amen.

Fifth Sunday in Lent

Lections: Isaiah 43:16-21; Psalm 126; Philippians 3:4b-14; John 12:1-8

Invocation

O God, today again
Let your Spirit come with conviction and cleansing.
Wash us with the pure water of repentance.
Turn our faces to Christ in true faith.
Keep us from putting any confidence in the flesh.
Give us hearts of obedience and love,
And a deep desire to know Christ in all his fullness.

Benediction

"To this end we always pray for you, asking that our God will make you worthy of [God's] call and will fulfill by [God's] power every good resolve and work of faith, so that the name of our Lord Jesus may be glorified in you, and you in him, according to the grace of our God and the Lord Jesus Christ" (2 Thess. 1:11-12).

Passion/Palm Sunday

Lections: Isaiah 50:4-9*a*; Psalm 118:1-2, 19-29; Philippians 2:5-11; Luke 19:28-40

Invocation

Merciful God,
Forgive our faltering faith,
And our lack of love, for you and others.
Our Lord has told us to follow in his steps,
In servanthood and sacrifice.
Yet we fail so often to follow,
And we steer clear of suffering for his name's sake.
As we come to worship, show us our Savior upon the cross.
Renew our faith and love,
Show us your mercy,
And give us your enabling grace.
Through Jesus Christ our Lord.

Benediction

We know the love of God
Because Christ lay down his life for us.
Go forth, as Christ's followers,
Walking in his steps.
Loving, in deed and truth,
And the peace of God will go with you.

Easter Season

Easter Day

Lections: Acts 10:34-43; Psalm 118:1-2, 14-24; 1 Corinthians 15:19-26; John 20:1-18

Invocation

O merciful God, we praise you, we worship you, we thank you! On this holy day we gather to worship in the name of Jesus by whose death and Resurrection we have been redeemed. Upon each person gathered here, let your blessings rest. Renew your church in this place and throughout the world as your people assemble in praise and gratitude for this Resurrection Day. In the name of the risen Lord, we pray. Alleluia! Amen!

Benediction

Go from this place in celebration because you have heard of God's great plan of salvation for humankind. Go in joy because the living Jesus has redeemed you! Go in trust and hope because the Holy Spirit guides you. Go in remembrance because this is the day of Resurrection. Christ has risen! (Christ has risen, indeed.)* Amen.

Second Sunday of Easter

Lections: Acts 5:27-32; Psalm 118:14-29; Revelation 1:4-8; John 20:19-31

Invocation

You are our God and we give you thanks.
You are our God and we praise you.

---

*Words in parentheses indicate congregation's response.

O Lord, in your death and Resurrection,
You have opened to us the gates of right living,
the glad songs of victory, and
the promise of eternal life.

Thank you for answering our longing to be one with you.
You are our God and we give you thanks.
You are our God and we praise you.

Benediction

This is the day that the Lord has made.
Let us continue in it,
With our gladness and rejoicing,
Honoring our risen Savior.
Alleluiah!

Third Sunday of Easter

Lections: Acts 9:1-6, (7-20); Psalm 30; Revelation 5:11-14; John
21:1-19

Invocation

O God, Creator of the universe
And the giver of all good,
We praise you for the love
Shown in our Savior, Jesus Christ.
He came from glory.
He died, rejected on a cross.
He rose, triumphant from the dead.
Because he lives, we live.
Because he lives, we are here today
To worship and to call upon your name.
We wait upon your blessing.

Benediction

"Now may the God of peace, who brought back from the dead our Lord Jesus, the great shepherd of the sheep, by the blood of the eternal covenant, make you complete in everything good so that you may do [God's] will, working among us that which is pleasing in [God's] sight, through Jesus Christ, to whom be the glory forever and ever. Amen" (Heb. 13:20-21).

Fourth Sunday of Easter

Lections: Acts 9:36-43; Psalm 23; Revelation 7:9-17; John 10:22-30

Invocation

Today, O God, we rejoice
To join with those in heaven,
And the millions around the world
Who join in worshiping you,
To sing the songs of the ages
That declare our faith,
To pray and praise with the saints of all time,
Inspired by your Holy Spirit,
To honor Christ who is King of Kings,
Lord of the church, who is alive forevermore.

Benediction

As you go from this place of united worship,
Go, knowing that the Good Shepherd
Goes with you.
Go, knowing that all heaven is on your side,
To urge you onward
To lift you heavenward,
To strengthen you always,
Wherever you go.

Fifth Sunday of Easter

Lections: Acts 11:1-18; Psalm 148; Revelation 21:1-6; John 13:31-35

Invocation

We gather as your people to worship you, O God. Call our wandering minds to think your thoughts. Draw our divided loyalties to hear your call as Lord. Lift our hearts in true praise to you,
Our Savior and Deliverer,
Our Sustainer and Comforter,
Our Lord and our God.
Then fill us with such love
That everyone we meet
Will know assuredly, that we are Christ's disciples.

Benediction

And now, as you go from this place of worship,
Go with the presence of the resurrected Christ,
Go with the power of the Holy Spirit,
Go with the Word of God dwelling in you richly,
Go with the love for one another, which Christ commands,
And the love of God,
The joy of the Holy Spirit,
The peace Christ gives,
Will be yours.

Sixth Sunday of Easter

Lections: Acts 16:9-15; Psalm 67; Revelation 21:10, 22–22:5; John 14:23-29

Invocation

Today, O God, as we gather, we pray
Come as holy light to enlighten our minds.

Come as holy truth to teach us your way.
Come as holy wind to blow a fresh work of your Spirit.
Come as holy fire to cleanse us from all sin.
Come as holy power to send us into your service.

Benediction

"May the Lord make you increase and abound in love for one another and for all. . . . May [God] so strengthen your hearts in holiness that you may be blameless before our God . . . at the coming of our Lord Jesus with all his saints" (1 Thess. 3:12-13).

Seventh Sunday of Easter

Lections: Acts 16:16-34; Psalm 97; Revelation 22:12-14, 16-17, 20-21; John 17:20-26

Invocation

Lord of the church, we call upon you as your people. Today, as we gather, mold us into a true spiritual and physical body of Christ. We cannot imagine what it would be like without the church, the leaven of righteousness, the good news of salvation from sin, the loving hands reaching out to others. Thank you that you are presiding over your church through all adversity and all the temptations of prosperity and poverty. Today, in this worship hour, help us to respond as your people, so that the world may believe and know that you love each person and you have sent Christ, the Savior.

Benediction

"The LORD our God be with us, as [God] was with our ancestors; may [the Lord] not leave us or abandon us, but incline our hearts to [God], to walk in all [God's] ways, and to keep [God's] commandments, . . . statutes, and . . . ordinances, which [God] commanded our ancestors. . . . So that all the peoples of the earth may know that the LORD is God; there is no other" (1 Kings 8:57-58, 60).

Season After Pentecost

Trinity Sunday
(First Sunday After Pentecost)

Lections: Proverbs 8:1-4, 22-31; Psalm 8; Romans 5:1-5; John 16:12-15

Invocation

It's scary, Lord, to look into the far reaches of space—without you! It's lonesome, Lord, to probe the pages of time past—without you!
It's terrifying, Lord, to peer into the unknown future—without you!
But what is most frightening of all, Lord, is to be here NOW,
Without you!
We beg you, Lord, come into our presence.
Assure us that your love has fixed the boundaries of space and time.
And grant us faith to cherish the majesty and comfort of your name in
this present moment. Amen.

Benediction

We've caught a glimpse today, O Lord, of your majesty.
The patterned clockwork of your infinite universe
Gives witness to your Glory.
The first words of babies,
And the presence of love in our lives
magnify your majesty!
Strengthened, we step confidently into tomorrow,
rejoicing that your presence
will guide us into all truth. Amen.

Sunday Between May 29 and June 4 Inclusive (if after Trinity Sunday)

Lections: 1 Kings 18:20-21, (22-29), 30-39; Psalm 96; Galatians 1:1-12; Luke 7:1-10

Invocation

O God, in your mercy and love
Redeem us from our lostness,
Restore us from our brokenness,
Release us from our bondage,
Receive us into your family,
Renew us by your Word and Spirit
Through Jesus Christ our Lord.

Benediction

"Grace to you and peace from God our Creator and the Lord Jesus Christ, who gave himself for our sins to set us free from the present evil age, according to the will of our God and Creator, to whom be the glory forever and ever. Amen" (Gal. 1:3-5).

Sunday Between June 5 and June 11 Inclusive (if after Trinity Sunday)

Lections: 1 Kings 17:8-16, (17-24); Psalm 146; Galatians 1:11-24; Luke 7:11-17

Invocation

O God of the universe, you are so mighty and yet you care for us so tenderly. Thank you for your great love that embraces both men and women, rich and poor, single people and those with families, people of different ages, people of different ethnic backgrounds and religious traditions, people who live in different parts of the world. May your never-ending love so fill our lives and worship that we might freely share your love with others. Amen.

Benediction

Trust God for the past—for the forgiveness of past sins, the healing of past hurts. Trust God for the present—for meeting daily needs, for guidance in daily living. Trust God for the future—for help with tomorrow's troubles, for the hope of eternal life. In a world of uncertainty, God's love is sure. Past, present, and future—God's love remains forever. Amen.

Sunday Between June 12 and June 18 Inclusive (if after Trinity Sunday)

Lections: 1 Kings 21:1-10, (11-14), 15-21*a*; Psalm 5:1-8; Galatians 2:15-21; Luke 7:36–8:3

Invocation

Today, O God, we are grateful
For the faith that sustains us,
For the hope that inspires us,
For the light that guides us,
For the love that comforts us,
For the forgiveness that frees us.
Above all, O God,
We are grateful for your only Son
Who, by his life, death, and Resurrection,
Made faith, hope, light, love, and forgiveness
A reality today.

Benediction

Let us go from here, living by the faith of Christ
Who gave himself for us.
Let us leave with his forgiveness
And with the gift of forgiveness
To all persons.
And the joy and peace of Christ
Will be with you.

Sunday Between June 19 and June 25 Inclusive (if after Trinity Sunday)

Lections: 1 Kings 19:1-4, (5-7), 8-15*a*; Psalm 42 and 43; Galatians 3:23-29; Luke 8:26-39

Invocation

Almighty God,
You are the one who comes.
As the deer longs for streams of water,
So our souls long for you, O God.
Enable us to see and hear you,
Even in the sound of utter silence.
May your presence bring healing,
Hope, and deliverance to us,
Your people this day. Amen.

Benediction

Go in the strength of God,
Which overcomes our weakness.
May the power, peace, and presence of Jesus Christ
Uphold, direct, and keep you always. Amen.

Sunday Between June 26 and July 2 Inclusive

Lections: 2 Kings 2:1-2, 6-14; Psalm 77:1-2, 11-20; Galatians 5:1, 13-25; Luke 9:51-62

Invocation

Our God of mercy and grace, in this hour,
Pour out your mercy and grace in our lives,
Until we take on your likeness.
You are light—shine into our hearts.
You are goodness—deliver us from evil.
You are love—fill us with compassion.
You are power—give us divine enablement.
You are full of forgiveness—make us able to forgive.
Let your life flow through us,
Even as you live within us, through your Spirit.
We pray in the name of Jesus.

Benediction

For freedom Christ has set you free.
Let us leave this place
With the deep assurance that Christ is able
To break every form of bondage.
And Christ will, through his Spirit,
Fill your life with love.
Go forth in the freedom and love of Christ.

Sunday Between July 3 and July 9 Inclusive

Lections: 2 Kings 5:1-14; Psalm 30; Galatians 6:(1-6), 7-16; Luke 10:1-11, 16-20

Invocation

We come O God
With a thirst for your presence.

Put within us the impulse for prayer.
Pull from us every grip of pride.
Free us from fear.
Help us kneel in our need
And to rise in your strength.
May we willingly become part of that body,
Of forgiveness and instruction,
Wherein our Lord is again made flesh
And dwells on the earth.

Benediction

Let your benediction of blessing rest upon our dear ones and our friends, wherever they may be today. Go with us to our homes and our work. And give us that kind of spirit that will not forget your presence with us always. Remove every form of pride or self-deception that would cause us to look with disdain on another. Enable us to be persons of reconciliation and restoration, as we go in the peace and love of our Lord Jesus.

Sunday Between July 10 and 16 Inclusive

Lections: Amos 7:7-17; Psalm 82; Colossians 1:1-14; Luke 10:25-37

Invocation

We come to you, O God,
As those whom you have rescued
From the power of darkness
And transferred
Into the kingdom of your beloved Son,
In whom we have redemption,
The forgiveness of sins.
We come in worship and praise, for your love for us.
And we pray that today we may deeply desire

To share all you have done for us
With others who have not yet experienced
Your deliverance and gifts.

Benediction

May you "lead lives worthy of the Lord, fully pleasing to [God], as you bear fruit in every good work and as you grow in the knowledge of God. May you be made strong with all the strength that comes from [God's] glorious power, and may you be prepared to endure everything with patience, while joyfully giving thanks to the Creator, who has enabled you to share in the inheritance of the saints in the light" (Col. 1:10-12).

Sunday Between July 17 and July 23 Inclusive

Lections: Amos 8:1-12; Psalm 52; Colossians 1:15-28; Luke 10:38-42

Invocation

We come to you, O God
Our Creator, Redeemer, and Sustainer.
We seek to magnify you and praise you as we ought.
We want to see Jesus in whom all of your fullness dwells.
We invoke your presence with us.
You are the giver of all we have
And our hope for now and hereafter.
May the memory of your goodness
And love you lavish on us, through Jesus Christ,
Fill our hearts with true gratitude and joy
As we worship today.

Benediction

Go from here
To the work and witness of life
Knowing that the living Christ
Goes with you.
And may Christ himself
Present you holy and unblamable
And unreproachable in God's sight.

Sunday Between July 24 and July 30 Inclusive

Lections: Hosea 1:2-10; Psalm 85; Colossians 2:6-15, (16-19); Luke 11:1-13

Invocation

Let this day, O Lord, which you have made and given to us, be a day of gladness and joy. We bless and honor you in this house dedicated to your glory, to worship and to praise your name.
Today we praise you for the privilege of prayer. And as we pray and as your Word is preached—
Send forth your Word so that we may hear your will.
Send forth your light so that we may see your way.
Send forth your Spirit so that we may be empowered to follow.
May we, in response to your invitation to pray, ask, search, knock, receive, and find. Through Jesus Christ our Lord. Amen.

Benediction

"Now unto him that is able to do exceeding abundantly above all that we ask or think, according to the power that worketh in us, Unto him be glory in the church by Christ

Jesus throughout all ages, world without end. Amen" (Eph. 3:20-21 KJV).

Sunday Between July 31 and August 6 Inclusive

Lections: Hosea 11:1-11; Psalm 107:1-9, 43; Colossians 3:1-11; Luke 12:13-21

Invocation

O living God, as we turn to you, we turn from old habits and old patterns, casting them aside like an old coat that's suddenly become too small. We turn from pride to seek a new humility, from greed to find compassion, from complaining to show forgiveness. Even as we worship this morning, transform our lives, clothe us in your love. In the name of Jesus, who gives us new life. Amen.

Benediction

Turn to the Lord, and receive God's blessing:
In this world of confusion, God will guide your steps;
When you stumble and fall, God will lift you up;
When you are too tired to take another step,
God will carry you and give you new strength.
Blessed be the Lord God, the Holy One in our midst. Amen.

Sunday Between August 7 and August 13 Inclusive

Lections: Isaiah 1:1, 10-20; Psalm 50:1-8, 22-23; Hebrews 11:1-3, 8-16; Luke 12:32-40

Invocation

Give to us the seeing of the eyes of faith.
Give to us the knowing of the renewed mind.
Give to us the believing of the surrendered heart.
Give to us the purity that desires beyond ordinary perception.
Give to us the goal that is the essence of your purpose.
Give to us the faith that trusts in your complete provision,
To each of us as we pray
In the name of Jesus. Amen.

Benediction

As you go from here, go forth in faith.
Go, joining the faithful of all ages,
Who labored long,
Who suffered much,
Who rejoiced greatly.
Go forth. Go forth in faith,
Knowing God created us for a purpose,
Loves us with a steadfast love,
Cares for us above all creation
And the peace of God shall go with you.

Sunday Between August 14 and August 20 Inclusive

Lections: Isaiah 5:1-7; Psalm 80:1-2, 8-19; Hebrews 11:29–12:2; Luke 12:49-56

Invocation

O God, in our worship today
We would join the long line of witnesses
To your faithfulness and love.
Help us learn from these to be faithful.

Through your searching Word and Spirit
Speak to us regarding those hindrances
That keep us from complete commitment.
Enable us to remove them from our lives.
Lift our eyes until we see Jesus
As he is—the author and finisher of our faith.
Open our hearts to receive him fully as Lord and Savior.
For it is in his name we gather and pray this prayer.

Benediction

Go from here as God's people.
Look at the witnesses of the past
And find good encouragement for your journey.
Look out for the hindrances that so easily overtake you.
Above all, look unto Jesus.
He is the perfect one and the perfecter of your faith.

Sunday Between August 21 and August 27 Inclusive

Lections: Jeremiah 1:4-10; Psalm 71:1-6; Hebrews 12:18-29;
Luke 13:10-17

Invocation

We praise you, O God, our Creator and Redeemer. We thank
you for this day with its overarching goodness and grace that
come from your hand. May this hour of worship be like
streams in the desert that provide joy, beauty, and refreshment. We gather with a variety of experiences and expecta-
tions; even so, we are confident that you can hear the
longings of our hearts. We worship you in adoration and
praise. Your grace is near us in the calm and in the storm: We
wait before you seeking to discern your holy will and desir-

ing to be a faithful church of Jesus Christ, our Lord. In his name we pray. Amen.

Benediction

As you depart from one another, may you go with joy and care for your brothers and sisters. May you encourage one another in Christian discipleship, prayer, and service. And may the love and grace of God through Jesus Christ make you a holy people for God's honor and glory. Amen.

Sunday Between August 28 and September 3 Inclusive

Lections: Jeremiah 2:4-13; Psalm 81:1, 10-16; Hebrews 13:1-8, 15-16; Luke 14:1, 7-14

Invocation

Today, O God, we join our lives and hearts in worship. Let the hearts of all those who seek you rejoice. Let us, as your people, remember the wonderful works you have done and are doing. Give us thankful and believing hearts so that our faces may always be turned toward you with praise and our feet may always follow in the footsteps of Christ who calls us to be his disciples of love and compassion.

Benediction

Let us continually offer the sacrifice of praise to God,
the fruit of our lips that confess God's name.
Let us continue to do good at every opportunity and share what we have, knowing that every sacrifice is pleasing to God.

Sunday Between September 4 and September 10 Inclusive

Lections: Jeremiah 18:1-11; Psalm 139:1-6, 13-18; Philemon 1-21; Luke 14:25-33

Invocation

Lord our God,
You set before us life and death, blessings and curses.
Rescue us from sinful paths;
Teach us to choose your way,
to delight in you,
to meditate on your law,
and to love you more than life itself.
In this hour of worship
plant us beside your living stream so that we may hold
fast to you
And live all our days in righteousness and peace.
Amen.

Benediction

Like trees beside a stream whose leaves do not wither,
may God make you fruitful.
May God strengthen you to choose what is right
and turn you from wrong.
May God bless you and give you peace. Amen.

Sunday Between September 11 and September 17 Inclusive

Lections: Jeremiah 4:11-12, 22-28; Psalm 14; 1 Timothy 1:12-17; Luke 15:1-10

Invocation

Lord God,
We believe you are the same yesterday, today, and
forever.
We believe that you continue to love the lost and
wandering.
We believe that you rejoice over everyone who repents.
Come among us and in your mercy and love,
Redeem us from our lostness.
Rescue us from our wanderings.
Restore us from our brokenness.
Release us from our bondage.
Receive us into your family.
Through Jesus Christ, our Lord and Savior.

Benediction

Gracious God, you have come to us, in Christ
And have shown us your love, grace, and compassion.
As we go from here
Give us your patience when people are indifferent;
Give us your compassion when people are in need;
Give us your love to reflect your grace and forgiveness.
Through Jesus Christ, our Lord.

Sunday Between September 18 and September 24 Inclusive

Lections: Jeremiah 8:18–9:1; Psalm 79:1-9; 1 Timothy 2:1-7;
Luke 16:1-13

Invocation

O Comforter in sorrow, we are so in need of prayer.
We do not know how to be good stewards of your world.

We invade one another's space, we disrespect and reduce to rubble the contributions of our elders; we fight with our neighbors and waste one another's possessions. We squander our inheritance and abuse our powers.

Over and over, we seem to disregard what is holy until it is too late.

This morning, Lord, show us what we need to mourn more deeply.

Cut through our denial so that we can heal.

Lord, we ask this even though we may hate to cry or find it hard

To respect tears. We pray through Jesus Christ, our comforter and Lord. Amen.

Benediction

As we go from here, we say thank you, Lord, for giving us a good earth,

A home that is balanced and bountiful when well-managed.

Thank you, Lord, for the knowledge wise leadership requires.

We praise you for the degree to which our power has been distributed

Justly in our community. Thank you for Jesus whose death invites us to confess sin and to yearn for forgiveness.

Bless us this week with an eye and an ear for boundary violations

And grant us a new spirit of respect and peace.

Sunday Between September 25 and October 1 Inclusive

Lections: Jeremiah 32:1-3a, 6-15; Psalm 91:1-6, 14-16; 1 Timothy 6:6-19; Luke 16:19-31

Invocation

Guide our thoughts, O Lord,
that they may be filled with the knowledge of your
presence.
Guide our words, O Lord,
that all who hear them are drawn closer to you.
Guide our actions, O Lord,
that you are evident in all we do or leave undone.
(The last paragraph may be sung by a soloist or invite the congre-
gation to join you, if it's familiar.)
May the words of our mouths
And the meditation of our hearts,
Be acceptable in your sight, O Lord. Amen.

Benediction

God has been with us, guiding our thoughts,
inspiring our words, and reviving our spirits.
Go in the knowledge that God will love the chance
to accompany each of your thoughts, words, and actions,
as this next week unfolds.
May the words of our mouths and the meditation of our
hearts
be acceptable in your sight, O Lord. Amen.

Sunday Between October 2 and October 8 Inclusive

Lections: Lamentations 1:1-6; Lamentations 3:19-26 or Psalm
137; 2 Timothy 1:1-14; Luke 17:5-10

Invocation

Eternal and ever present God,
As you have made us and called us,
With a holy calling,

So guide and sustain our lives,
In your way and Word,
That our walk may be consecrated
To the building of your kingdom,
And our worship and work
May be one.
We ask this in the name of our Lord Jesus.

Benediction

"I commend you to God and to the word of his grace, which is able to build you up and to give you the inheritance among all those who are sanctified" (Acts 20:32 RSV).

Sunday Between October 9 and October 15 Inclusive

Lections: Jeremiah 29:1, 4-7; Psalm 66:1-12; 2 Timothy 2:8-15; Luke 17:11-19

Invocation

Gracious and merciful God,
You who pour out abundant blessings upon us,
we give thanks for all your great works.
Your righteousness endures forever;
You nourish the faithful; you make justice;
You uphold your covenant.
Holy is your name. Receive our worship today
As we offer the prayers of our hearts
And the songs of our lips,
For we are your grateful children.
Through Jesus Christ our Lord. Amen.

Benediction

Like Naaman who gave thanks when he was restored to
health,
and like the tenth leper who returned to praise God when he
was healed,
go forth with thankful hearts
for the power at work within you.
Endure hardship with patience,
and trust the mercy and grace of your Lord.
Live as true servants of Jesus Christ! Amen.

Sunday Between October 16 and October 22 Inclusive

Lections: Jeremiah 31:27-34; Psalm 119:97-104; 2 Timothy
3:14–4:5; Luke 18:1-8

Invocation

Speak to us Lord God.
We have come to hear your Word proclaimed.
Convince us of our sin
And your forgiving grace.
Rebuke our pride and selfishness
And replace them with humility and love.
Encourage our hesitant faith
And increase our confidence,
In your eternal truth.
Make this hour
A time and call to such commitment
That each may go from here equipped for every good work,
For your glory and the glory of Christ Jesus, our Lord.

Benediction

And now, go forth from here. "Be steadfast, immovable, always excelling in the work of the Lord, because you know that in the Lord your labor is not in vain" (1 Cor. 15:58).

Sunday Between October 23 and October 29 Inclusive

Lections: Joel 2:23-32; Psalm 65; 2 Timothy 4:6-8, 16-18; Luke 18:9-14

Invocation

O Lord, we invoke your presence and blessing.
You are the source of spring and autumn rains,
God of planting, and of the completion of harvest.
We acknowledge your power to stay the course through all seasons.
We cannot say the same about ourselves.
We are a people prone to wandering away from your path
And to forgetting our mission.
Lord, we want to fight the good fight, to finish the race, and to keep faith.
O Lord Jesus, source of spring and autumn rains, shower us with your mercy
For we are a people like warriors overcome in battle.

Benediction

God of life, go with us now. Thank you for pouring out your Spirit upon us.
You have blessed us with the waters of baptism.
You have given us, a community of believers, the joy of worshiping together.
You have created us, sons and daughters, old and young, living together.

You, O Christ, have always been with us
And especially when we have felt isolated, rejected, de-
spised, and ashamed.
Thank you for renewing a right spirit within us
And thank you for the peace that passes all understanding.

Sunday Between October 30 and November 5 Inclusive

Lections: Habakkuk 1:1-4; 2:1-4; Psalm 119:137-144; 2 Thessalonians 1:1-4, 11-12; Luke 19:1-10

Invocation

Lord, we're here, now, in this place.
By being here we proclaim that we are yours,
We wish to know more of you and your ways.
We seek direction from the Word, your communication to
us.
It tells us to live justly—
to defend the fatherless,
to plead the case of the widow.
It tells of Jesus' open acceptance of sinners such as
Zacchaeus,
Of Paul's thanks for and delight in people who also followed
you.
Today, bless your Word as it is spoken and taught.
Enable us to be faithful hearers and doers.

Benediction

Lord, hide your words in our hearts.
Bring them to consciousness as we walk the paths of
life.
Your Word brings wisdom and order into our existence—

It lights our way and expounds your love for us, your creation.
May we hide your Word in our hearts. Amen.

Sunday Between November 6 and November 12 Inclusive

Lections: Haggai 1:15*b*–2:9; Psalm 145:1-5, 17-21 or Psalm 98; 2 Thessalonians 2:1-5, 13-17; Luke 20:27-38

Invocation

As the darkness gives way to the dawn, O God,
Bring light into our lives today.
As the seed sprouts from the well-cared-for earth,
Bring life to your Word in our lives.
As the pure water quenches the thirst,
Pour the water of life into our lives.
We ask it in the name of Christ
Who is the light, the bread, and the water of life.

Benediction

"The LORD bless you and keep you;
the LORD make [God's] face to shine upon you, and be gracious to you;
the LORD lift up [God's] countenance upon you, and give you peace" (Num. 6:24-26).

Sunday Between November 13 and November 19 Inclusive

Lections: Isaiah 65:17-25; Isaiah 12; 2 Thessalonians 3:6-13; Luke 21:5-19

Invocation

Lord, your creative power is everlasting.
Even when fires, wars, revolutions
And unaccountable violence destroy
Everything that we have built,
Your loving intention of a world without harm remains in place.
Thank you, God, for your sustaining interest in us.
Lord, we ask for a strengthening of our tired bones and flagging spirits.
Help us to focus on our work so that we are a part of creating a new earth.
O Lord, your creative power is never-ending. You, O Christ, are unfailing.

Benediction

Hardworking God, as we leave this place,
We praise you for giving us life,
For meaningful work,
For food, shelter, our families, good health.
Thank you for giving us a big vision for this world.
If we lack for any good thing, bless us with the courage and energy
To do what we can
And the faith to leave the rest in your hands. Through Jesus Christ, our Lord. Amen.

Reign of Christ/ Christ the King Sunday

Lections: Jeremiah 23:1-6; Luke 1:68-79; Colossians 1:11-20; Luke 23:33-43

Invocation

Our God

We rejoice that you have brought us to the beginning and brightness of another Lord's day. We come because we need you and we pray that the presence of the living Christ may permeate this place.

May we be made strong with all the strength that comes from your glorious power! Prepare us to endure everything with patience, while joyfully giving thanks to you, our God.

You have enabled us to share with the saints in light. You have rescued us from the power of darkness. You have transferred us into the kingdom of your beloved Son. In him we have redemption, the forgiveness of sins.

Make these great truths real to each person present, to the glory and praise of your holy name.

Benediction

And now, all glory to the One who alone is God, who saves us through Jesus Christ our Lord; yes, splendor and majesty, all power and authority are God's.

Special Days
of the
Christian Year

CHRISTMAS DAY

Lections: Isaiah 9:2-7; Psalm 96; Titus 2:11-14; Luke 2:1-14 (15-20)

Invocation

Lord God, you have revealed to us
Your nature, your love in the incarnation of your Son,
Who lived among us,
Who shared our struggles,
Who won the victory over sin and death.
We come in gratitude today.
Speak to us, O God, especially today.
Keep us from becoming calloused with the familiar Christmas story.
Give us the meekness of those who came
From near and far to kneel in a lowly stable, to adore the Christ Child.
In Christ's birth and life we see your grace and truth.
In Christ's death we see your love.
In Christ's Resurrection we see your acceptance of his sacrifice,
And the assurance of our acceptance into your family.

Benediction

Now go forth from here
And may the Spirit of Christ go with you every moment.
May peace on earth and goodwill toward all persons
Be your experience and the experience of all Christ's disciples.

NEW YEAR'S DAY

Lections: Ecclesiastes 3:1-13; Psalm 8; Revelation 21:1-6*a*; Matthew 25:31-46

Invocation

O Lord God, you have brought us to a new year,
The start of a new journey,
With its freshness and potential.
You are the alpha and the omega,
The beginning and the ending.
We invite you into our worship
And into our lives,
So that, as we begin,
And as we end this year,
We can say,
"We have walked with you, O God.
"We have loved our Savior more."

Benediction

Go from here forgiven through Christ.
Enter the new year cleansed and made whole.
Go forth in the calm confidence
That the one who has called you
Will also go with you, both now and evermore.

Invocation

Lord God, we face the new year, with the promise of your presence.
You call us to ventures untried, paths untrodden, and perils unknown.
Come, guide us and empower us, so that we may live
Knowing that this year too shall swiftly pass,
And, at its close, we shall, with others, say "Already."
Give us each day
Some work to accompany our lives,
Some suffering to sanctify our spirits,
Some good to do in comforting others.
Give to us the Spirit of our Lord Jesus
Throughout the coming days and year.

Benediction

Go from here,
At the start of this new year,
Knowing that as God calls you
He will also enable you,
Knowing that Christ goes with you,
For he has promised he will never leave you.
Go in the name and blessing of Christ Jesus, our Lord.

ASH WEDNESDAY

Lections: Joel 2:1-2, 12-17; Psalm 51:1-17; 2 Corinthians 5:20*b*–6:10; Matthew 6:1-6, 16-21

Invocation

On this Ash Wednesday
We come to worship and to bow down
Before our God
Of creation, of salvation, of vocation.
Let us come before our God
Confessing our need
Of inner cleansing.
Let us come
Asking God to search us and try us
And to see if there is any wicked way
Within us.
Come with repentance that is real.
Come pleading our God
To purify our purposes,
To forgive our fallenness,
To restore the joy of our salvation,
And to leave again,
Assured of God's presence and power,
And as witnesses of God's love.

Benediction

Go from here
Believing that the Lord
Has heard your petitions,
That the Lord will guide you continually
And satisfy your needs
In parched places.
God shall make you strong
And you will be like a spring of water
Refreshing others
For God goes with you.
Amen.

PALM SUNDAY

Lections: Isaiah 50:4-9*a*; Psalm 118:1-2, 19-29; Philippians 2:5-11; Matthew 21:1-11

Invocation

We gather, O God,
With remembrance and with rejoicing,
In the vision and knowledge of Jesus
As he journeyed into the Holy City.
We gather and we pray
That Christ, the Lord of all,
Will ride on to reign,
In each of our lives,
As we lift our hearts and voices in praise.
Forgive our divided loyalties.
Purify and accept our praises and hosannas,
As we seek to offer them today
In the name of our King, Jesus.

Benediction

As you go from here, remember the parade of praise,
The meaning of Christ's Lordship,

In all your life and labor,
In the tough decisions of each day,
And Christ shall go with you.

WEDNESDAY OF HOLY WEEK

Lections: Isaiah 50:4-9*a*; Psalm 70; Hebrews 12:1-3; John 13:21-32

Invocation

Even as we invite your presence among us this Holy Week, O Christ, we are conscious that, like your first disciples, you are always coming to us and we fail to discern what you are saying. We too often have missed your clear words of warning and guidance. We confess that we also have denied you in the hour of trial. Forgive, forgive we pray.

Make this hour, this week, yes the rest of our lives, the time to hear your words, to know the true meaning of your suffering and death and the reality of your Resurrection. Then make us faithful witnesses to your glory, O Christ, we pray.

Benediction

"Go forth from here
To join the great cloud of witnesses,
To lay aside every weight and the sin that clings so closely,
To run with patience the race set before us.
Looking unto Jesus the author and finisher of our faith" (Heb. 12:1-2 paraphrased).

HOLY THURSDAY

Lections: Exodus 12:1-4, (5-10), 11-14; Psalm 116:1-2, 12-19; 1 Corinthians 11:23-26; John 13:1-17, 31*b*-35

Invocation

We meet today as those first disciples,
Delighting in your presence with us,
And yet, quickly aware of our petty natures,
Our desire for greatness and to be served, rather than to be servants.
We take hope in that you are present, O Christ,
To teach us again and again,
Your way in all relationships, to God and to one another.
By the power of your Spirit
Make us into your likeness, O Christ.
In loving compassion,
In humble service,
In obedient lives.

Benediction

Go from here, knowing that Christ's way is not in seeing how many serve us, but in seeing how many we serve. And, "may the Lord be generous in increasing your love and make you love one another and the whole human race. . . . And may he so confirm your hearts in holiness that you may be blameless in the sight of our God and Father when our Lord Jesus Christ comes with all his saints" (1 Thess. 3:12-13 JB).

GOOD FRIDAY

Lections: Isaiah 52:13–53:12; Psalm 22; Hebrews 10:16-25 or Hebrews 4:14-16; 5:7-9; John 18:1–19:42

Invocation

O God,
We know something of the true way of blessedness
Revealed and realized in Christ.
We see his suffering and death—
The path of love that led to the cross.
We see the reward of obedience

158

That led to a crown of thorns.
Forgive us when we have taken
Christ's sacrifice lightly
Or failed to rejoice in our salvation.
Teach us to take our cross and to follow in faith.
May we share the Savior's sorrow for sin
And know the secret of his strength
Each day, and hour, and moment. Amen.

Benediction

Let us go from here as Christ's disciples,
denying ourselves,
taking up our cross.
And following our Lord in Resurrection life.

HOLY SATURDAY

Lections: Job 14:1-14; Psalm 31:1-4, 15-16; 1 Peter 4:1-8; Matthew 27:57-66 or John 19:38-42

Invocation

Sovereign God, we are grateful
The tomb did not hold the Lord of glory.
The guards did not keep Christ within.
The seal did not secure the Savior.
Death and hell were not victorious.
Come to us in this hour of remembrance.
Give us again the vision
Of our Lord's suffering, death, and victory.
And seeing your deliverance
May we not falter or fail
To put our trust in you.

Benediction

"Since therefore Christ suffered in the flesh, arm yourselves
also with the same intention . . . so as to live for the rest of

your earthly life no longer by human desires but by the will of God. . . . The end of all things is near; therefore be serious and discipline yourselves for the sake of your prayers. Above all, maintain constant love for one another, for love covers a multitude of sins" (1 Pet. 4:1-2, 7-8).

EASTER VIGIL

Lections: Genesis 1:1–2:4*a*; Psalm 136:1-9, 23-26; Exodus 14:10-31; 15:20-21; Exodus 15:1*b*-13, 17-18; Romans 6:3-11; Psalm 114; Matthew 28:1-10

Invocation

O God, we gather this special hour.
We pray forgive when we have lived
As if Christ were not alive,
When we shared our faith
In timid tones
Rather than in robust and victorious voice.
Bring us to such belief in Resurrection reality
That our murmuring ceases
And all fear gives way to trust.
Fill life with the fragrance of faith,
The radiance of hope,
And the sunlight of love.
Raise us to newness of life
Through the living Christ.

Benediction

"May the God of hope fill you with all joy and peace in your faith, that by the power of the Holy Spirit, your whole life and outlook may be radiant with hope" (Rom. 15:13 JBP).

Invocation

Praise to you, O God,
You raised up your Son our Savior

From the dead and gave him glory,
Giving us faith and hope in you.
Praise be to you, O Christ,
You are the Resurrection and the Life.
And by your glorious Resurrection
You brought life and immortality to light.
Praise to you, O Holy Spirit,
You shed abroad the love of Christ,
In our hearts,
And made us rejoice in the hope of glory.
All praise, thanks, dominion, and power
Be unto you, blessed trinity, now and forever more.

Benediction

Eternal Savior, we have seen in your victory
Our hope realized, our faith confirmed, our strength renewed.
As we go from here
May the victory of the risen Christ be our victory.

EASTER EVENING

Lections: Isaiah 25:6-9; Psalm 114; 1 Corinthians 5:6b-8; Luke 24:13-49

Invocation

O God,
Open our eyes to see
You have opened for us the gate to eternal life
By the Resurrection of Christ our Lord.
Open our minds to understand
The significance of Christ's life
So that even in suffering
We may know the joy of life indeed.
Like the disciples, who walked sadly to Emmaus,
Cheer and warm our hearts

By the presence and power of Christ.
Sustain us in the faith, that as he lives
So shall we live now and forever.

Benediction

"And now may the God of peace, who brought again from the dead our Lord Jesus, equip you with all you need for doing his will. May he who became the great Shepherd of the sheep by an everlasting agreement between God and you, signed with his blood, produce in you through the power of Christ all that is pleasing to him. To him be glory forever and ever" (Heb. 13:20-21 TLB).

ASCENSION OF THE LORD

Lections: Acts 1:1-11; Psalm 47; Ephesians 1:15-23; Luke 24:44-53

Invocation

O God, as we gather on this special day to remember the ascension of our Lord, we know his leaving was not the end of his ministry. It was a new beginning. And like this story of our Lord's ascension is at the beginning of the book of Acts, so also the message of the angels, "stop gazing and start going," is the message we need to hear.

Yes, that was the beginning of a new relationship with you, O Lord, a relationship that did not depend upon vision or physical presence. It was also the beginning of a new responsibility, that of being empowered, guided, and blessed by the Spirit of Christ as his disciples went as witnesses to the ever reigning Christ.

Give us the vision of the living Christ and the continuing mission that has been given to us, his body, in the world today.

162

Benediction

Go forth from here in the power of the ascended Christ who said, "Go therefore and make disciples of all nations." Go with the presence of the ascended Christ who said, "I am with you always." Go with the purpose of the ascended Christ who assures you that he will confirm the message in the lives of all those who hear.

DAY OF PENTECOST

Lections: Genesis 11:1-9; Psalm 104:24-34, 35*b*; Acts 2:1-21; John 14:8-17, (25-27) (Year C)

Invocation

For the gift of your Spirit we praise you, O God.
And now we come to you by the Spirit's conviction.
We have new life through the Spirit's indwelling.
You have made us your children
By the Spirit's adoption.
We witness and serve
By the Spirit's empowerment.
We yearn to be more like Jesus
Because of the Spirit's urgings.
Continue your gracious work
So that we may walk in this world
Free from the bondage of sin
And free to do your will,
In the glorious liberty of your children
Through your Holy Spirit.

Benediction

You have been given the gift of the Holy Spirit.
Go forth empowered and equipped by the Spirit
To be Christ's body, doing Christ's work in the world.

Invocation

Today, O God,
As we join in united worship,
May each receive the regenerating work of your Spirit.
May each know the illuminating work of your Spirit.
May each experience the sanctifying work of your Spirit.
May each drink of the living water of your Spirit.
So that we may leave this place of worship,
The new creation that you intend,
Filled with your Holy Spirit,
To share the life of Christ
Wherever we go.

Benediction

God, in the name of the Lord Jesus,
The one who said, "Peace be with you.
As [God] has sent me,
So I send you."
Receive the Holy Spirit.
And go in the forgiveness of Jesus Christ.

Invocation

O God, welcome.
As all that you have for us is made a reality to us by your Holy Spirit, we thank you for the advocate you have given us. On this day of Pentecost we pause to pray our special gratefulness that Christ did not leave us alone, that he sent the Spirit of truth, of power, and enablement. Today we pray that we may surrender to the Holy Spirit as fully as we know, in order that Christ might be glorified in and through each believer. We ask it in the name of Jesus, our Lord. Amen.

Benediction

And now may the Spirit that was in Christ Jesus be in you enabling you to know God's will and empowering you to do God's will day by day and moment by moment.

Invocation

O Lord God,
Fill us afresh with the Spirit of that first Pentecost,
So that we may bear a willing and joyous witness
To Christ and his kingdom.
May our worship and witness be such
That we will hasten the day
When the knowledge of Christ
Shall encircle the earth
As the waters cover the sea.

Benediction

Go forth
Led by the Holy Spirit,
Conscious that you are God's children.
Go forth
As willing and joyful witnesses
To the living Christ,
Conscious that all the blessings of Christ's
Are yours also
Because you are God's family.

ALL SAINTS

Lections: Wisdom of Solomon 3:1-9; Psalm 24; Revelation 21:1-6*a*; John 11:32-44 (Year B)

Invocation

O God, we are called to come in worship before you.
And so we come. We pray that you will open the eyes of our hearts that we may know what is the hope to which you have

called us; that we may understand how rich and glorious is the inheritance in Christ, which is ours, together with all the saints; that we may understand the greatness of your power working through Christ, who has been raised to be Lord of all, who is seated far above all other powers, above every name, for this age and for the age to come.
Open our eyes. Open our hearts. Open our understanding. God of glory, God of our Lord Jesus Christ, show to us the mystery of yourself. Reveal to us your eternal purpose for your people.
We hope in you. We praise your glory. Amen.

Benediction

May your blessing, O God, be upon us this day, as it has been on all the saints who have come before us.
May your blessing be upon the poor, the hungry, and the wretched of our world. Fill the hungry, enrich the poor, and comfort the marginalized. Bring to all the riches of your glorious inheritance of hope, of power, and of love.
May your blessing be upon all those who will yet hear the Word of truth, who will yet put their hope in Christ our Lord. Together with all the saints everywhere, may we come to know you ever more deeply. May we live each day ever closer to your ways, in love, forgiveness, and compassion. Amen.

Invocation

Alpha and Omega,
    our beginning and our end,
    You rejoice at the birth of your children;
    You weep when we stand bereft beside a grave.
Come among us today, strong and mighty Lord,
As we remember and give thanks for all your saints.
Wipe away the tears from our faces
    and show us your glory,
    For we wait upon your grace. Amen.

Benediction

May God who makes all things new
dwell among us
and give us life. Amen (based on Rev. 21:1-6*a*).

THANKSGIVING DAY

Lections: Deuteronomy 26:1-11; Psalm 100; Philippians 4:4-9;
John 6:25-35 (Year C)

Invocation

"Come, thou fount of every blessing."
Pardon the forgetfulness and ingratitude with which we
receive our daily blessings. Come and move by your Holy
Spirit within us even while we pray, that our praises and
thanksgivings may overflow in happy song and joyful life.
Make this day and the worship so real to our hearts that we
may go forth in life filled with gratitude and not taking life
for granted ever again.

Benediction

Go from here.
Be thankful always.
Have gratitude in your hearts to the Lord.
Let your life overflow with praise.
And the God of all love and grace,
The giver of every good and perfect gift,
Will fill your life with happy songs of joy.

VARIOUS OCCASIONS

Invocation

O God of love,
Come among us in this hour of worship
So that we may learn again
How to receive your love.
Reveal any blocks we may have

In believing or receiving your love.
Then, having sensed your love,
Send us forth as sharers of your love,
With all whom we meet.

Benediction

Go forth, assured of God's love
Revealed supremely in sending God's Son
To be our Savior.
Go forth, sharers of Christ's love,
In home, in work, and in play.
Go forth knowing that God, who is love,
Goes with you.

Invocation

We come today out of our aloneness,
With a longing to know you, O God.
Though present already,
According to your promise,
Give us such a sensitivity to your Spirit,
That, as we meet,
And, as we leave again,
Each of us may say
"Surely God was in this place,
And we need never be alone.
For Christ goes with us."

Benediction

Go forth from here,
As those who experience Christ's love,
As ambassadors of Christ's love,
Ministering to people in their aloneness.
Break through fear and isolation
In the ministry and miracle
Of reconciliation, through Christ,
To all you meet.

Invocation

O God, our Creator and Redeemer,
May your presence be so real among us

That we may bow in reverence,
Worship with true praise,
Pray with sincere thanksgiving,
And receive from you
All you desire to impart.
Give us a love for you,
And your truth,
So that we may truly know you
And, by your truth,
We may be made free.

Benediction

Go forth from this time of worship
As witnesses to the living Christ,
Fearlessly extending Christ's kingdom
Wherever we may move.

Invocation

Almighty God,
As ages ago you spoke
And brought order out of chaos,
Speak again in our troubled times
And let "our ordered lives confess
The beauty of thy peace."
As you brought light out of darkness,
Shed your light
Upon our lives
So that we may see clearly
To follow Christ
Who is the light of the world.

Benediction

Go forth from here,
With the Word as a lamp to your feet,
And as a light to your pathway.
Go forth, with your face,
Always toward Christ,
Who is the light of the world
Who goes before you.

List of Contributors

Sandra Drescher-Lehman, of Richmond, Virginia, is a professional social worker and counselor. She is also the author of numerous books, including *Just Between God and Me*, *Meditations for New Moms*, and *Waters of Reflection*.
Writer of pp. 12*a*, 34, 43, 52, 60*a*, 75*b*, 92*b*, 113, 123*b*, 142.

Duane E. Frederick is pastor of the Meadow Mountain Mennonite Church in Swanton, Maryland.
Writer of pp. 19, 31, 41, 79*b*, 107.

Larry Hauder, of Boise, Idaho, is the Conference Overseer for the Pacific Northwest Mennonite Conference.
Writer of pp. 27, 40*b*, 49, 84, 114.

Phoebe Hershey is a computer professional who is involved in a clinical pastoral education program that works with the elderly in Washington, D.C., and Maryland. She resides in Silver Spring, Maryland.
Writer of pp. 16, 50, 80, 118, 165*b*.

Marlene Kropf is Minister of Worship and Spirituality for the Mennonite Board of Congregational Ministries. She also teaches at Associated Mennonite Biblical Seminary in Elkhart, Indiana.
Writer of pp. 33*a*, 69*b*, 140*a*, 144, 166.

Maurice Martin, of New Hamburg, Ontario, Canada, is a former secondary school teacher. He currently teaches at the Blenheim Bible Study and Retreat Center, and is a pastor.
Writer of pp. 15, 23, 37, 79*a*, 104*a*.

Jane Peifer is co-pastor at Community Mennonite Church in Harrisonburg, Virginia. She is also a writer, and is the co-author of *Welcoming New Christians*.
Writer of pp. 10, 22*a*, 53, 85, 120.

Lois Janzen Preheim is a teacher, writer, and pastor. She also serves as Director/Mediator for the Victim Offender Reso-

lution Program of Sioux Falls, South Dakota.
Writer of pp. 35, 103, 141, 146, 148*b*.

Emma Richards is a retired teacher, and a former missionary
to Japan. She also served for many years as a pastor in the
Chicago area. She currently resides in Goshen, Indiana.
Writer of pp. 9*a*, 39, 110*a*, 123*a*, 138.

Earl Sears is the pastor of Faith Mennonite Church in New-
ton, Kansas.
Writer of pp. 29, 44, 119*a*.

Edith Shenk, of Harrisonburg, Virginia, serves as associate
pastor of Weavers Mennonite Church. She is also a peer
counselor for a pregnancy center and is a hospital chap-
lain. She and her family served as missionaries in east
Africa for eighteen years.
Writer of pp. 14*b*, 46, 78, 116, 147.

Ervin Stutzman, of Mt. Joy, Pennsylvania, is a bishop and
moderator of the Lancaster Mennonite Conference. He is
the author of *Being God's People, Creating Communities of the
Kingdom*, and *Welcome*.
Writer of pp. 66, 71, 74*b*, 99, 131.

April Yamasaki, of Abbotsford, British Columbia, Canada,
is pastor of Emmanuel Mennonite Church. She is the
author of *Where Two Are Gathered* and *Remember Lot's Wife
and Other Unnamed Women of the Bible*.
Writer of pp. 28*a*, 62*b*, 86*b*, 92*a*, 129*b*, 136*a*.

Robert Zehr serves as pastor of Des Allemands (Louisiana)
Mennonite Church. He is the District Overseer for Gulf
States Mennonite churches. He is also a pilot.
Writer of pp. 22*b*, 36*b*, 40*a*, 45*b*, 58, 62*a*, 81, 97, 109, 128.

All remaining Invocations and Benedictions were written by
the compiler and editor, John M. Drescher.

Index of Scriptural Passages

INDEX

INDEX